FORTIES FABRICS

Joy Shih

Schiffer Publishing Ltd

77 Lower Valley Road, Atglen, PA 19310

To Jeanne
We laugh in the face of bad design

On title page:
From *Sears Catalog,* Spring and Summer 1941, Philadelphia, Edition 182, © **Sears, Roebuck and Co.**

Published by Schiffer Publishing Ltd.
77 Lower Valley Road
Atglen, PA 19310
Phone: (610) 593-1777
Fax: (610) 593-2002
E-mail: schifferbk @ aol.com

Please write for a free catalog.
This book may be purchased from the publisher.
Please include $2.95 for shipping.
Try your bookstore first.

We are interested in hearing from authors
with book ideas on related subjects.

Contents

Attack of the flying thimbles. Other colors, not shown, in
rose pink, aqua, yellow and French gray. Spring 1949.

From *Sears Catalog*, Fall and Winter 1938-39,
Boston, Edition 177, © **Sears, Roebuck and Co.**

INTRODUCTION

For most people the 1940s seem to appear in varied tones of black and white. We remember black and white photographs, black and white newspapers, black and white newsreels and movies, and for those lucky enough to have it, black and white television sets. During the first half of the decade a world war brought home stark images of weapons, machinery, airplanes and battleships. The latter half of the 1940s, with subsequent postwar reconstruction and worldwide political restructuring, were not exactly colorful experiences either. So it is not unusual to think of those times as drab and depressing.

Designers of the decade, however, did not give up on color. Witness the hundreds of bright and beautiful fabric designs on the following pages, many of them in interesting and eye-popping color combinations. Women who did most of the sewing continued to mob department stores whenever new shipments of colorful cloth arrived in order to provide their families with the latest fashion styles. Photographs from the era recorded a number of men in the crushing crowds, sent by excited women who could not attend themselves. Catalog pages from 1940s *Sears, Roebuck and Co.* jumped out in brilliant colors to entice consumers to purchase the latest designs in fabric to sew or in ready-to-wear clothing. Advertisements from textile manufacturers bragged about the color-retention qualities of their product, even when washed repeatedly. Everyday life overflowed with color, perhaps even more so in light of war times.

Lincoln, Nebraska department store's special Election Day sale. Women who couldn't get to the sale sent their men. 1946.

The designs in this book are actual fabric samples from leading textile manufacturers in the 1940s. All the swatches shown are made of cotton, a practical material for everyday wear and home use. Cotton was extremely popular and, most of all, affordable. Color trends and motifs reflected popular culture, which in turn was influenced by current events.

During the war years, for example, many designs appeared in American patriotic colors of red, white, and blue. Though other colors were available, the largest swatch in manufacturers' pattern books were often presented in red, white and blue. Color names such as *flag red*, *glory blue*, *cadet blue*, *aircorps blue*, *army tan*, and *navy* helped to bolster the consumer's sense of patriotism and of course, to encourage sales. Sailors, stars and stripes, and military motifs were popular images. Some of the muted color schemes during early decade were due to dyestuff that was diverted for the war effort.

Postwar colors shifted to a preference for chartreuse and rose tones and some designs began to show abstract shapes that would continue into the 1950s. Late decade designs became less "serious" and more "whimsical" in nature. Florals started to take on a less realistic look and moved to bolder prints, especially for use in the home. Geometrics became twisted and wavy and more adventurous.

An advertisement from a leading textile manufacturer, dated mid-1947, announced to readers of popular national magazines that "everyday clothes haved changed from gray to *gay*. Changed to colors that laughed at washday. And have you *seen* the good news? The clothesline tells it: We're back after a wartime scarcity. In bright bolts of ready-to-sew, *needlized* cloth. In clothes ready-to-wear for you and your family...daytime dresses, shirts, shorts, pajamas. Expertly styled. Finished with a perfection worthy of our quality."

In most cases, floral and geometric fabrics in the book are arranged not by subject matter or motif, but by pattern design. Florals, for example, are categorized by *allover packed* (non-directional pattern with very little or no background shown), *allover spaced* (non-directional pattern with more background showing), *monotone* (one color design), *monochromatic* (different tones of one color), or *two-tone* designs. Plaids are presented in checkered or *boxed* layout, *diagonal* pattern, or florals on plaid *ground* (background). To appreciate color trends, many designs are presented in other available *colorways* or background color. Novelty prints are arranged by subject or by their intended use as in *kitchen* design or *children's* designs.

I invite you to take a nostalgic tour of the decade's finest floral, geometric and novelty prints. May it surprise you and inspire you.

Geometric Designs

Checks: Gingham

From *Sears Catalog*, Spring and Summer 1941, Philadelphia, Edition 182, © **Sears, Roebuck and Co.**

An allover pattern of equal width stripes crossed at right angles is called a gingham check. Samples of small gingham checks. Spring 1941.

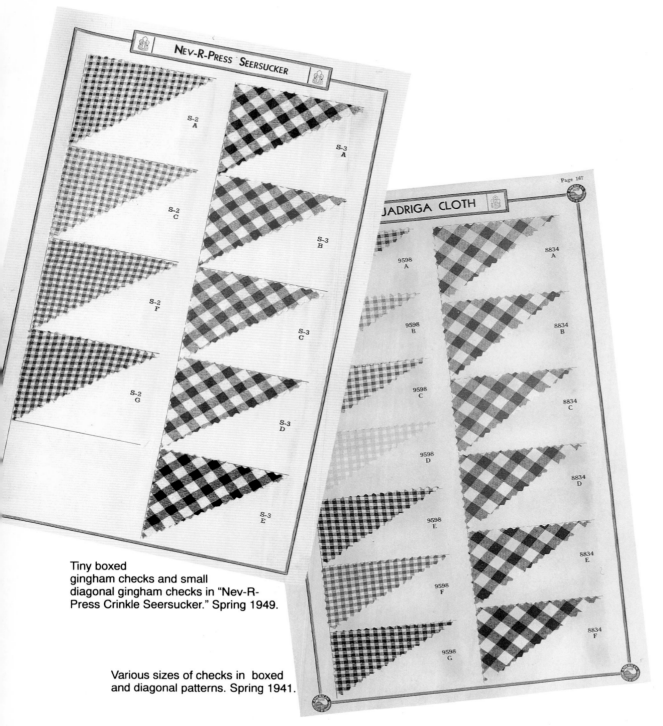

NEV-R-PRESS SEERSUCKER

S-2 A

S-2 C

S-2 F

S-2 G

S-3 A

S-3 B

S-3 C

S-3 D

S-3 E

Tiny boxed
gingham checks and small
diagonal gingham checks in "Nev-R-Press Crinkle Seersucker." Spring 1949.

Various sizes of checks in boxed
and diagonal patterns. Spring 1941.

JADRIGA CLOTH

Page 167

9598 A

9598 B

9598 C

9598 D

9598 E

9598 F

9598 G

8834 A

8834 B

8834 C

8834 D

8834 E

8834 F

From *Sears Catalog*, Fall and Winter
1948, Philadelphia, Edition 197,
© Sears, Roebuck and Co.

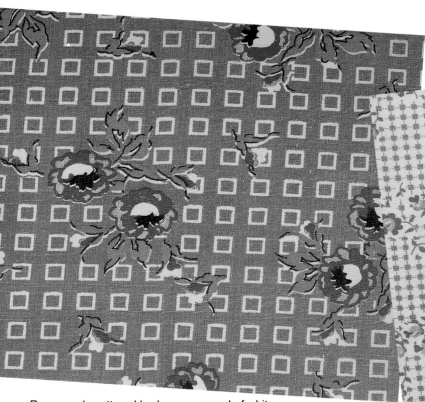

Roses and scattered buds on a ground of white outlined squares, forming a novelty checked pattern. Also colorways (background color), not shown, in rose pink, aquamarine, violet, and butter yellow. Spring 1941.

Interlocking circles of roses over an allover houndstooth-style patterned ground. Spring 1949.

CHECKS: FLORAL
IN BOXED LAYOUT

Tiny sprigs of flowers on double windowpane checks. The navy check pattern is placed over the white, creating smaller checks. Other colorways, not shown, are bright cherry pink, turquoise, butter yellow, and mocha tan. Spring 1941.

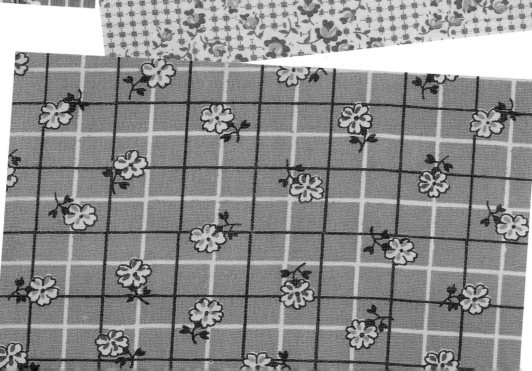

Sprigs and small floral clusters spaced on a tiny windowpane checks, two-directional pattern. The checked ground gives the fabric a denim look. Spring 1941.

10

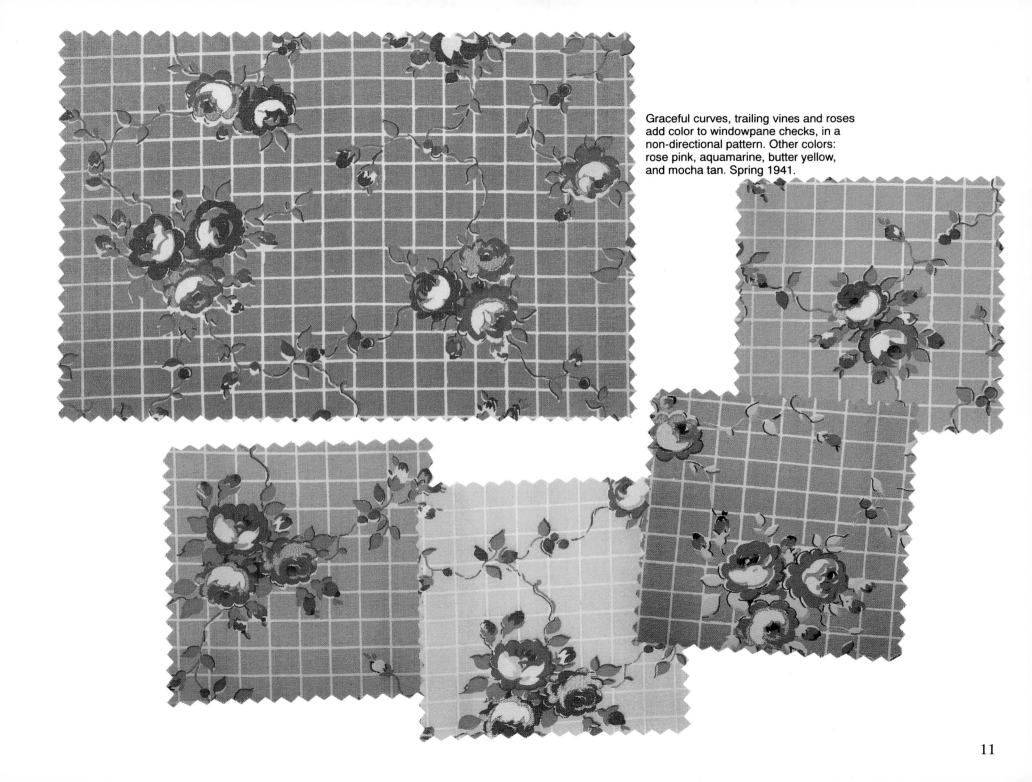

Graceful curves, trailing vines and roses
add color to windowpane checks, in a
non-directional pattern. Other colors:
rose pink, aquamarine, butter yellow,
and mocha tan. Spring 1941.

A single curled leaf in alternating boxed layout, in pastel shades. Spring 1949.

Scattered sprigs of flowers, encircled by wreaths of leaves, on windowpane checks. Also available, not shown, in pink, aquamarine, gray, and yellow colorways. Spring 1941.

A perfectly laid out garden design with slate-like shapes bordered by a floral and ribbon boxed pattern. Spring 1949.

A novelty checkered pattern in royal blue and dark cherry pink, kelly green and wine red, golden yellow and pepper green, burgundy and French gray. Spring 1949.

From *Sears Catalog*, Spring and Summer 1947, Boston, Edition 194, © **Sears, Roebuck and Co.**

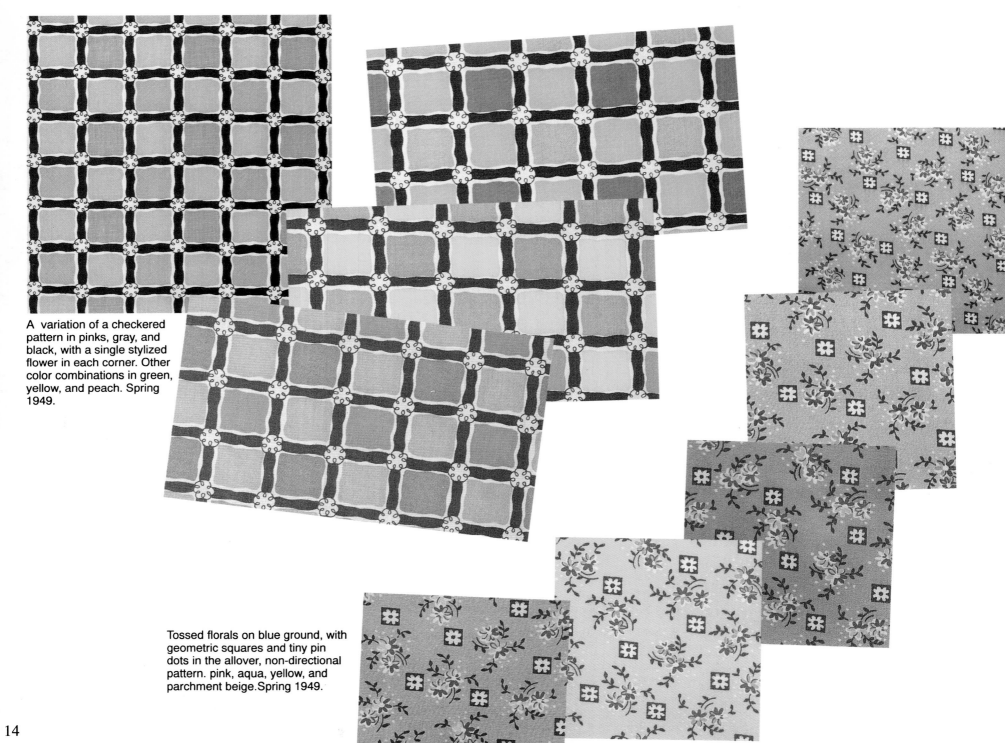

A variation of a checkered pattern in pinks, gray, and black, with a single stylized flower in each corner. Other color combinations in green, yellow, and peach. Spring 1949.

Tossed florals on blue ground, with geometric squares and tiny pin dots in the allover, non-directional pattern. pink, aqua, yellow, and parchment beige.Spring 1949.

14

Checks: Diagonal

Bowknots and snowflakes in a diagonal boxed layout. The wavy lines lend movement to the design. Fall 1948.

From *Sears Catalog*, Fall and Winter 1948, Philadelphia, Edition 197, **© Sears, Roebuck and Co.**

Diagonal checks pattern in subtle shades of beige, brown and aquamarine. Fall 1948.

Harlequin print in bright spring colors of dark rose pink, teal green, concord blue, and sand. The creative use of smaller and larger dots gives the pattern movement. Other colors combinations: bright cherry pink, lime green, dusty violet, dawn gray; cactus green, copen blue, emerald green, light blue; tangerine, nickel gray, rust, dawn gray; army tan, aquamarine, Bermuda green, light blue. Spring 1942.

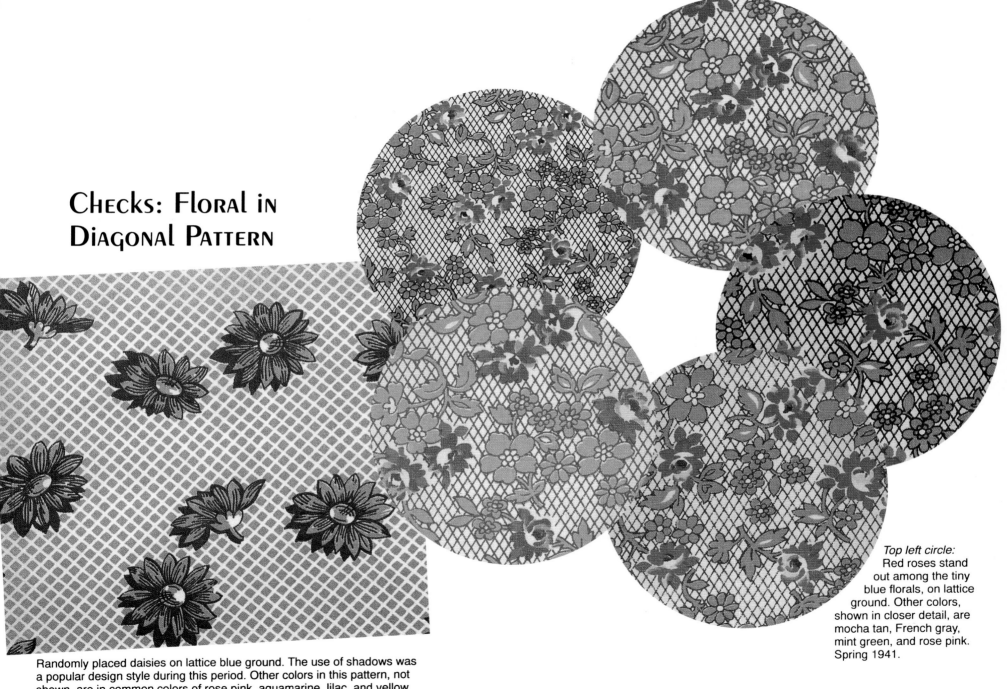

Checks: Floral in Diagonal Pattern

Randomly placed daisies on lattice blue ground. The use of shadows was a popular design style during this period. Other colors in this pattern, not shown, are in common colors of rose pink, aquamarine, lilac, and yellow.

Top left circle: Red roses stand out among the tiny blue florals, on lattice ground. Other colors, shown in closer detail, are mocha tan, French gray, mint green, and rose pink. Spring 1941.

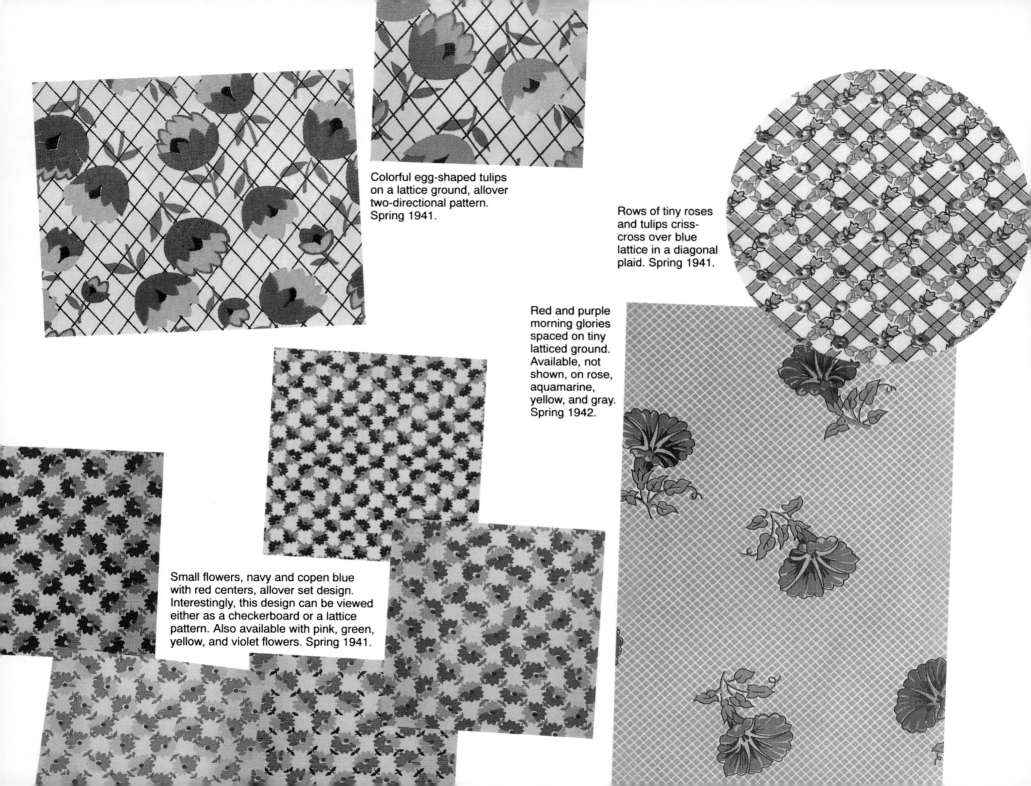

Colorful egg-shaped tulips on a lattice ground, allover two-directional pattern. Spring 1941.

Rows of tiny roses and tulips criss-cross over blue lattice in a diagonal plaid. Spring 1941.

Red and purple morning glories spaced on tiny latticed ground. Available, not shown, on rose, aquamarine, yellow, and gray. Spring 1942.

Small flowers, navy and copen blue with red centers, allover set design. Interestingly, this design can be viewed either as a checkerboard or a lattice pattern. Also available with pink, green, yellow, and violet flowers. Spring 1941.

Checks: Novelty

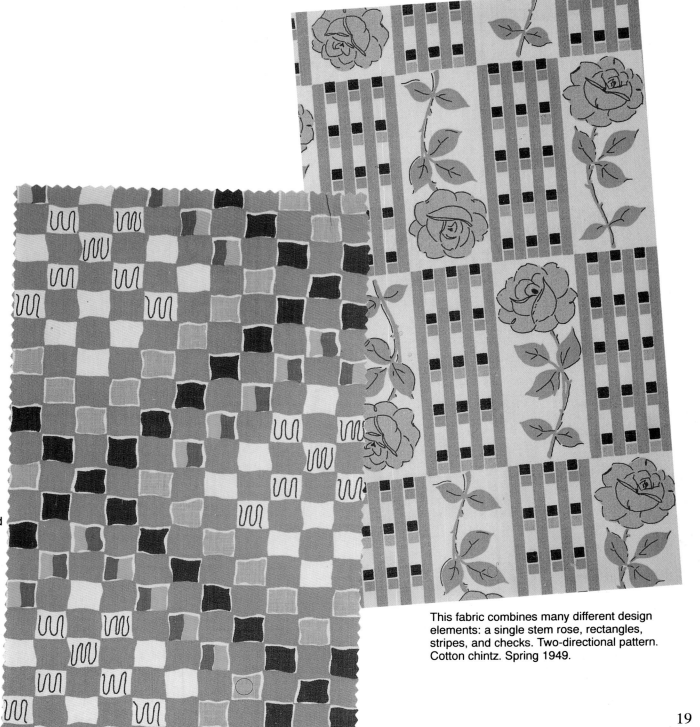

Wavy pastel checks combine with hairpin lines to form this interesting pattern. The black checks give the overall look of this design a diamond shape pattern. Spring 1949.

This fabric combines many different design elements: a single stem rose, rectangles, stripes, and checks. Two-directional pattern. Cotton chintz. Spring 1949.

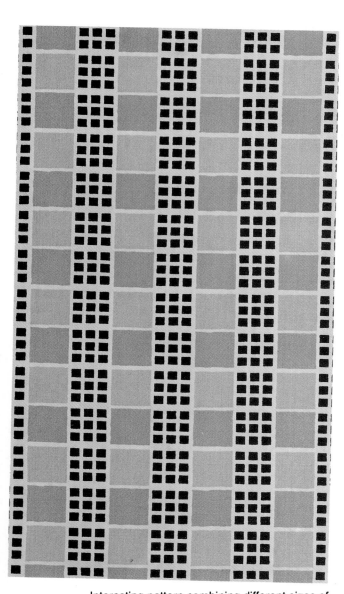

Interesting pattern combining different sizes of checks. The use of black sharply contrasts the pastel pink and blue, giving the impression of a stripe pattern. Spring 1949.

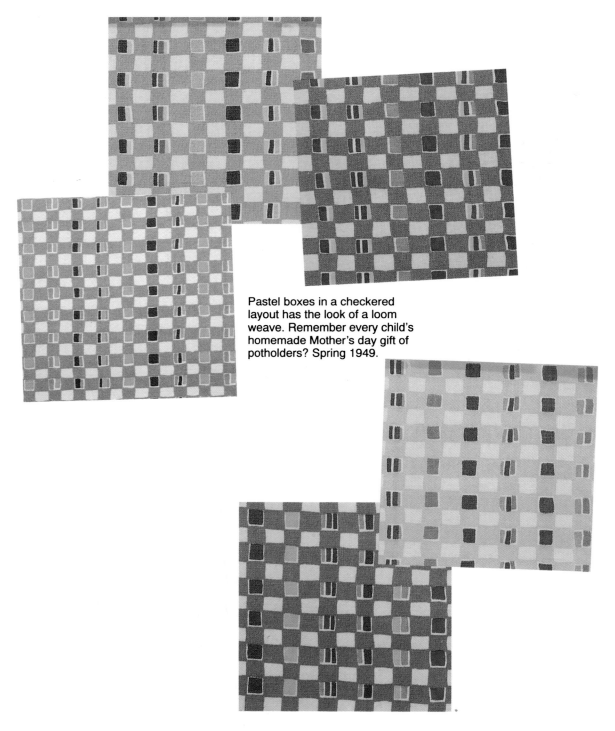

Pastel boxes in a checkered layout has the look of a loom weave. Remember every child's homemade Mother's day gift of potholders? Spring 1949.

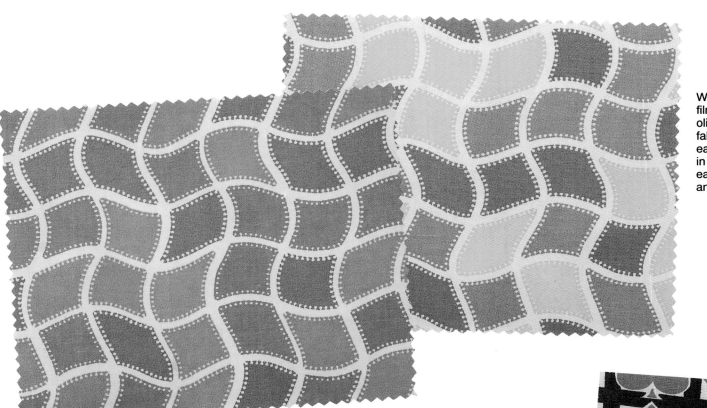

Wavy box layout with the look of celluloid film, in dark cherry pink, nickel gray and olive green. The use of olive green in fabric design, practically absent in the early part of the decade, became popular in the late 1940s and continued into the early 1950s. Shown also in yellow, blue, and slate gray. Fall 1948.

Playing cards motif in a bold box layout, two-directional pattern. Shown in red. Not shown, in copen blue, teal, yellow, and mocha tan. Spring 1949.

Northcoastal Native American motifs and fretwork are arranged in a box layout to create this colorful print. Fall 1948.

21

Plaid: Boxed Layout

Stripes criss-cross to form a check pattern. Other colors not shown: valley rose, aquamarine, violet, butter yellow. Spring 1941.

Large windowpane checks in bold colors placed over a subtle checked pattern creates a plaid design. Spring 1949.

Soft plaid with the look of flannel. Very thin cotton. Spring 1949.

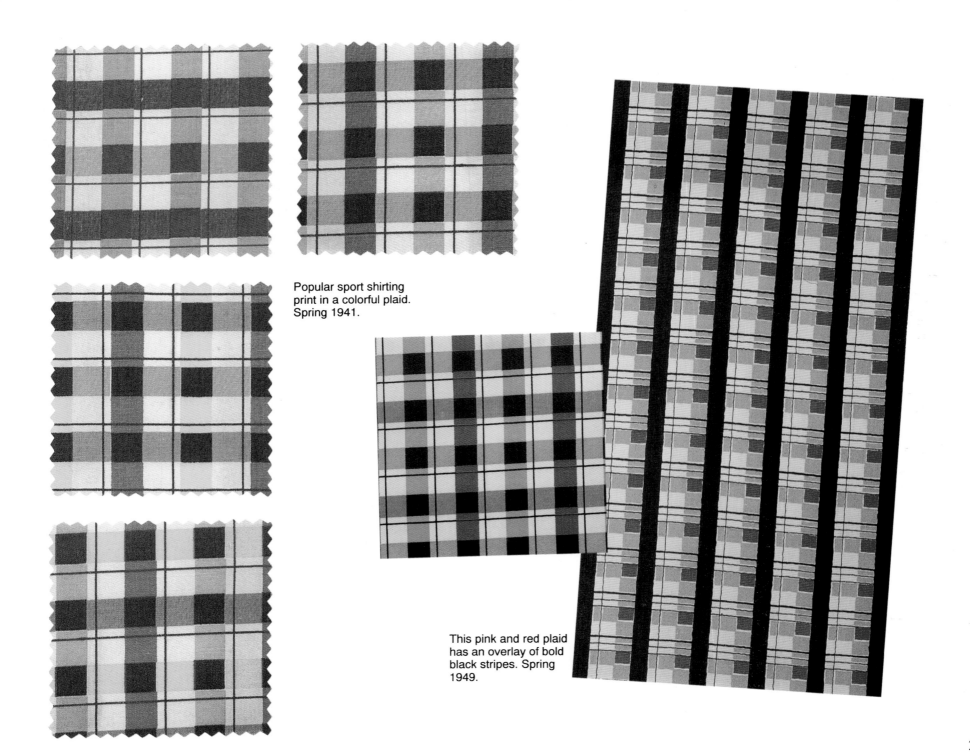

Popular sport shirting print in a colorful plaid. Spring 1941.

This pink and red plaid has an overlay of bold black stripes. Spring 1949.

23

Popular red, white and blue plaid
pattern featuring diamond-shaped
quatrefoils, with woven textured look.
Cotton chintz. Spring 1941.

Red, white and blue plaid with a
heavy woven look, printed on very
thin cotton. Spring 1941.

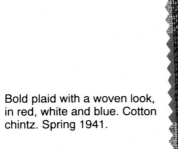

Bold plaid with a woven look,
in red, white and blue. Cotton
chintz. Spring 1941.

Aquamarine and pink stripes in a diagonal plaid pattern. Spring 1941.

Plaid: Diagonal

Very large bold plaid in a diagonal pattern. Spring 1941.

The overlapping of the diagonal box layout gives this pattern a three-dimensional look. Spring 1949.

Bright diamond print. The alternating navy lines in the diamonds give it a raised three-dimensional effect. Cotton chintz. Fall 1948.

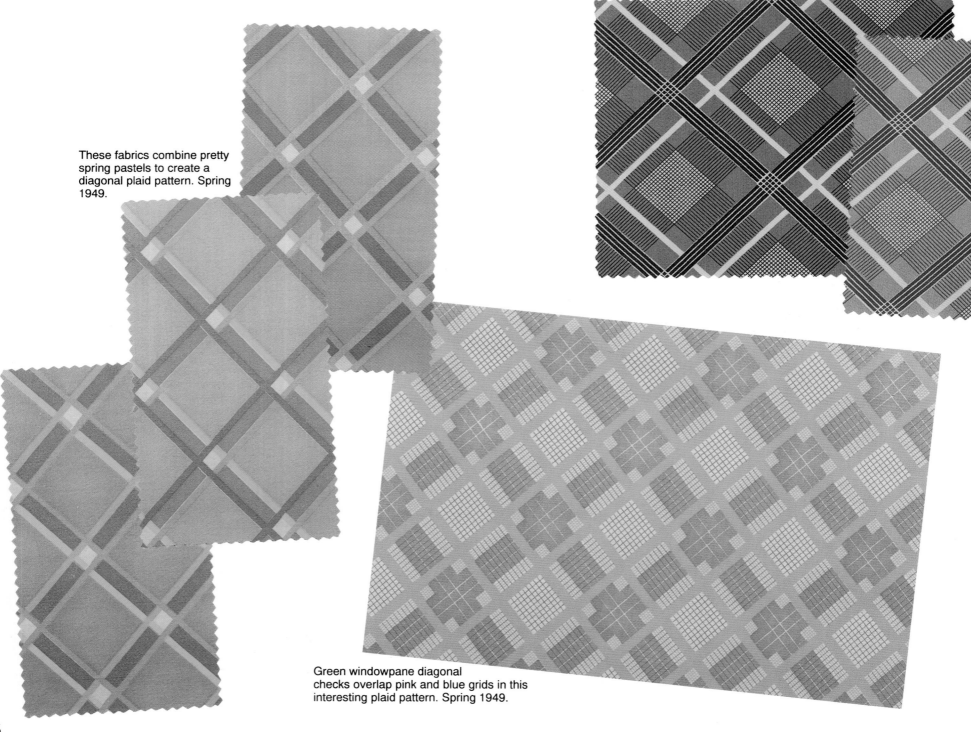

These fabrics combine pretty
spring pastels to create a
diagonal plaid pattern. Spring
1949.

Green windowpane diagonal
checks overlap pink and blue grids in this
interesting plaid pattern. Spring 1949.

26

Variation of a diagonal plaid. Note the bright blue and deep rose pinks popular during this period. Other colors, not shown, are aqua, desert sand, and yellow. Fall 1948.

A small diagonal plaid design in red, white and blue. Fall 1948.

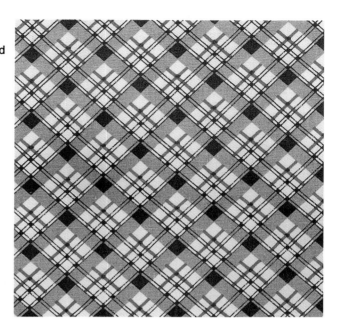

Variation of a diagonal plaid. Other colors not shown: pink, aquamarine, lilac, bright yellow. Fall 1948.

This busy diagonal plaid design is actually a check pattern. The dark blue lines suggest plaid. Spring 1949.

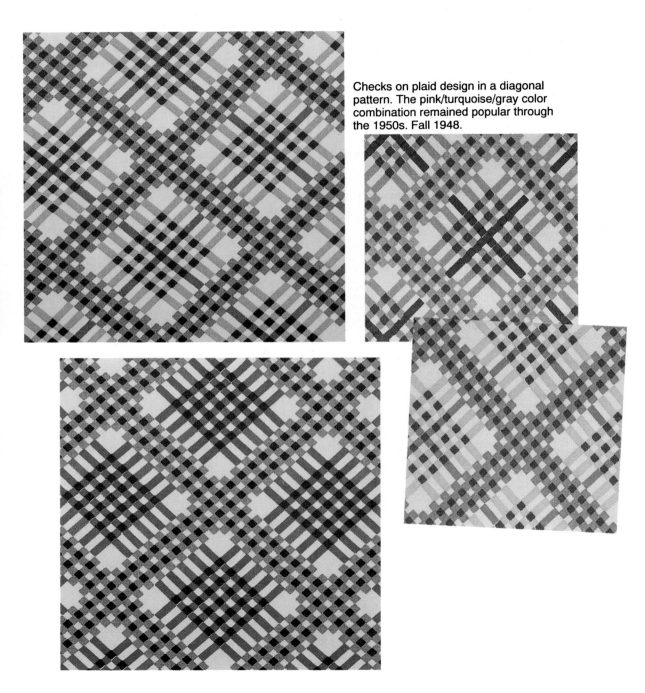

Checks on plaid design in a diagonal pattern. The pink/turquoise/gray color combination remained popular through the 1950s. Fall 1948.

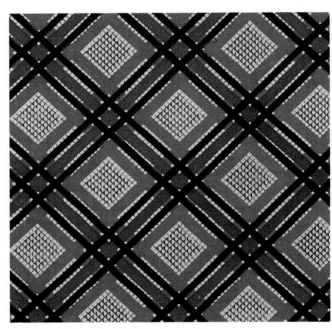

A unique diagonal plaid in not-so-unique colors of red, white and blue. The squares in the design features a common quilt pattern. Spring 1949.

Variation of the popular red, white and blue diagonal plaid design. Spring 1949.

A very bold plaid in red and black. Spring 1949.

Very popular plaid pattern in red, white and blue. The model wearing a dress made from this fabric appeared in an ad in the manufacturer's pattern book. Spring 1942.

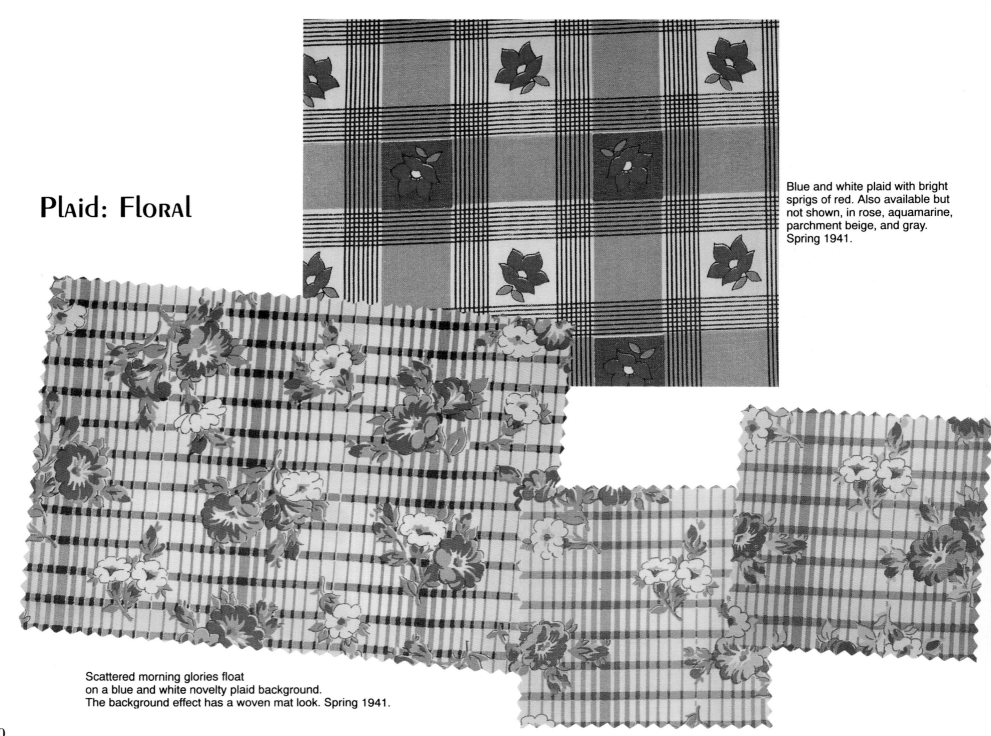

Plaid: Floral

Blue and white plaid with bright sprigs of red. Also available but not shown, in rose, aquamarine, parchment beige, and gray. Spring 1941.

Scattered morning glories float
on a blue and white novelty plaid background.
The background effect has a woven mat look. Spring 1941.

Large sprays of anemones on blue ground. Note the creative use of fine lines placed in unequal widths to give the illusion of "plaid". Spring 1941.

Pink version of the pattern. Also available in turquoise, lilac, and yellow colorways.

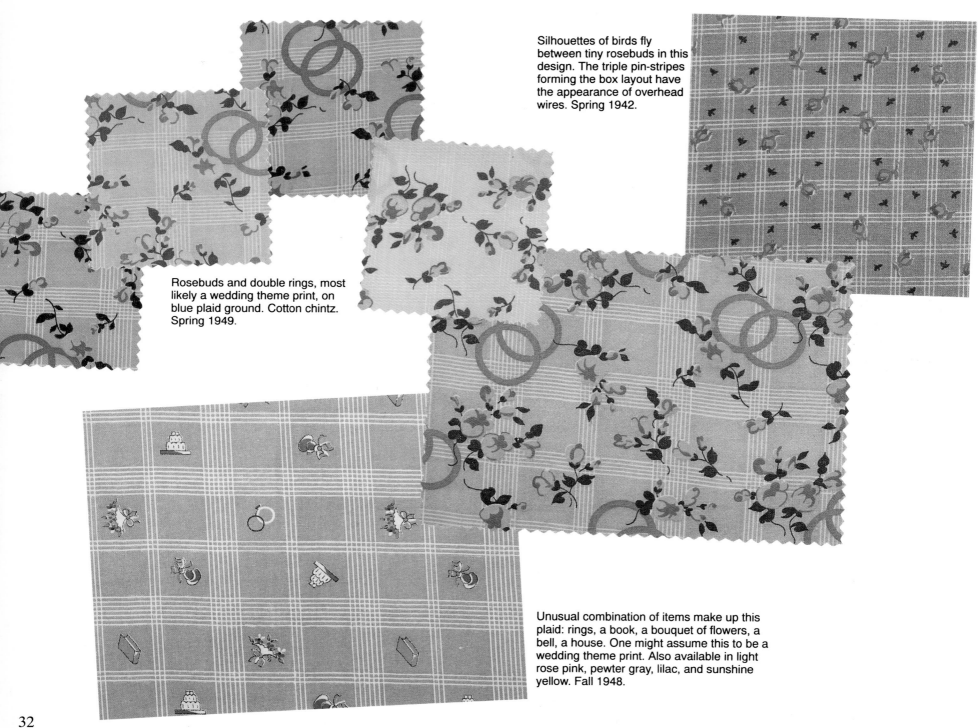

Silhouettes of birds fly between tiny rosebuds in this design. The triple pin-stripes forming the box layout have the appearance of overhead wires. Spring 1942.

Rosebuds and double rings, most likely a wedding theme print, on blue plaid ground. Cotton chintz. Spring 1949.

Unusual combination of items make up this plaid: rings, a book, a bouquet of flowers, a bell, a house. One might assume this to be a wedding theme print. Also available in light rose pink, pewter gray, lilac, and sunshine yellow. Fall 1948.

Tiny clusters of flowers on boxed layout formed by a leaf pattern. The thin blue lines bordering the boxes gives the design a three-dimensional effect. Other colors in the same pattern: rose, aquamarine, lilac, butter yellow. Spring 1941.

From *Sears Catalog*, Spring and Summer 1941, Philadelphia, Edition 182, © **Sears, Roebuck and Co.**

Scattered dogwood blossoms in boxed layout, criss-crossed with double lines of lace. Fall 1948.

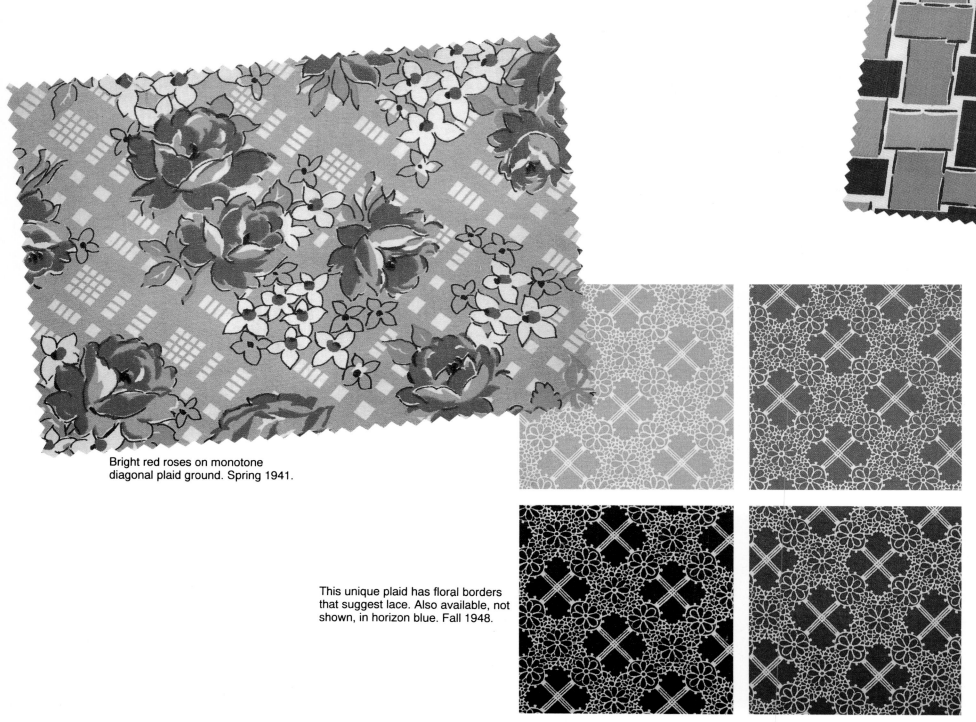

Bright red roses on monotone
diagonal plaid ground. Spring 1941.

This unique plaid has floral borders
that suggest lace. Also available, not
shown, in horizon blue. Fall 1948.

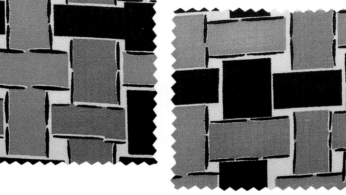

Bold basketweave design in browns and aquamarine. Note the deep shades in other color combinations of the same design. Fall 1948.

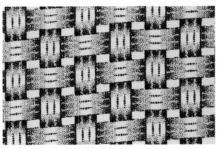

BASKETWEAVE

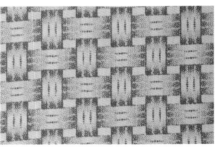

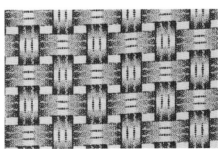

This trompe l'oeil basketweave design is a fine example of mill engraving, a printing technique using steel engraving to give fine detail and amazing texture to a smaller scale design. Spring 1949.

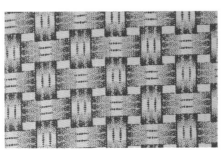

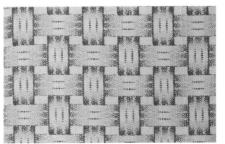

The use of the squiggly hairpin
lines in this novelty plaid creates
a basketweave look, in pastel
shades. Spring 1949.

Plaid: Novelty

A novelty diagonal
plaid where every line is wavy. The
random placement of scribbles gives the design an
unpredictable look. In gray, turquoise, and rose pink.
Spring 1949.

This design combines polka dots and stripes and
turns it into a diagonal plaid. Other colors: cherry
pink, mint green, pumpkin, navy. The use of red in
the navy pattern is particularly striking. Spring 1941.

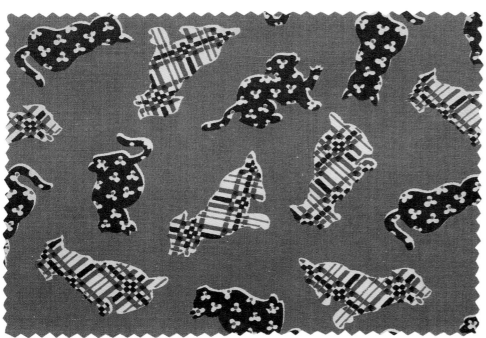

Calico cats and plaid dogs combine two
design elements into a whimsical print.
Other colorways: dark tapestry rose,
aqua, red, and navy. Spring 1941.

Stripes: Classic

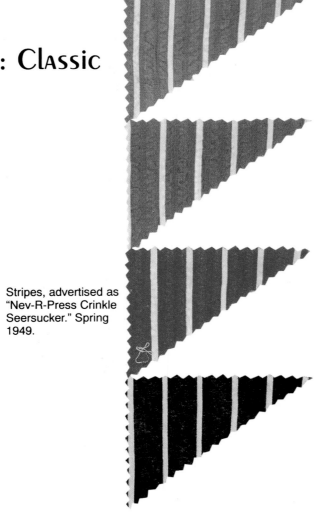

Stripes, advertised as "Nev-R-Press Crinkle Seersucker." Spring 1949.

S-

Closeup of seersucker fabric.

Another variation of the pink, gray, and black color combination in a very bold stripe pattern. Spring 1949.

Bright provincial stripes take its name from the colorful colors in folkwear originating in the French countryside of Provence. Spring 1941.

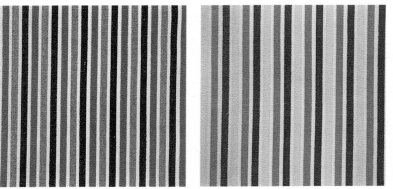

From *Sears Catalog*, Spring and Summer 1941, Philadelphia, Edition 182, © **Sears, Roebuck and Co.**

STRIPES: PROVINCIAL

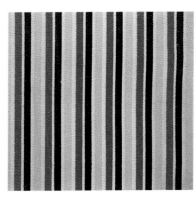

Spun Rayon Rambeline or Plain Color Rayon Poplin

Spun Rayon Rambeline

Spun Rayon Rambeline

Rayon Sharkskin or Rayon Poplin

"The low price of these dresses floored me," says Milt Weller. "I'm convinced that a girl can look smart without throttling her budget." And he's right!

"They're Beauties" $1.98 Each
Value $2.98

SAY MEN WHO SEE JUNIORS IN THEM!

2 for $3.89

Better quality Rayons for early Spring, or hot weather days; Rayons which are hand washable when given gentle Lux care

CHECKS—snappy casual dress vely. Rayon Sharkskin. Buttons Pocket-effects on front-shirred, ng skirt.

Size (Not Age) Range: 11, 13, 19. State size, color; Scale, oppo- re. Shipping weight, 1 lb. 2 oz. 113—Red-White, Copen-White or White checks............$1.98

(G) "HUGGER BELT" for lovely curves on a posy-print dress! Enameled zip-pleated bodice. Breezy gored skirt. All-Spun Rayon Rambeline.
Juniors' Size (Not Age) Range: 11, 13, 15, 17, 19. State size, color; Size Scale, opposite page. Ship. wt., 1 lb. 2 oz.
◆7 H 7019—Floral Print on Navy, Rose or Copen Blue grounds....$1.98

(J) "WHITE FLASH", front and back on a button-down princess dress! Cotton lace trim. Buckle-back belt. Skirt in full swing! Spun Rayon *Rambeline*.
Juniors' Size (Not Age) Range: 11, 13, 15, 17, 19. State size, color; see Size Scale, opposite page. Shipping weight, 1 lb. 2 oz.
◆7 H 7025—Clay Brown, Moss Green or Copen Blue 607, white insets........$1.98

(K) SUCCESS DRESS! Wear it with its own necklace or with your other acces-

Printed or Plain

(H) "TWO-PIECER" gives you a

Very bold multi-color, multi-size stripe pattern, in predominant colors of red, white and blue. Spring 1941.

39

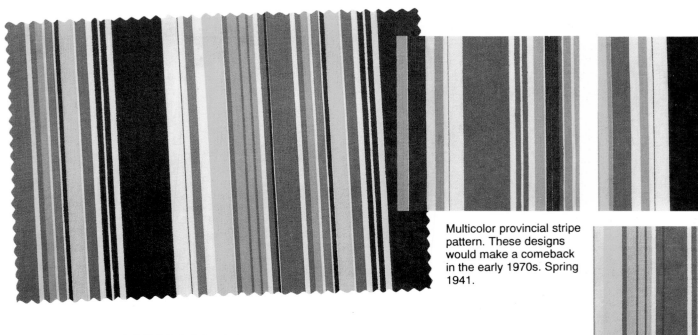

Multicolor provincial stripe pattern. These designs would make a comeback in the early 1970s. Spring 1941.

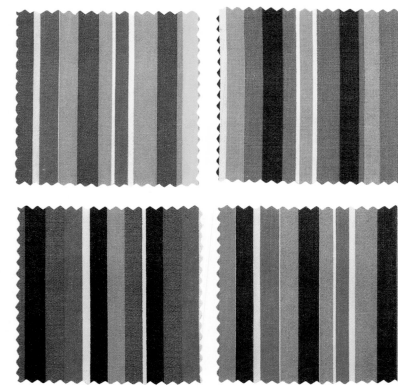

Provincial stripes in bright colors. Spring 1941.

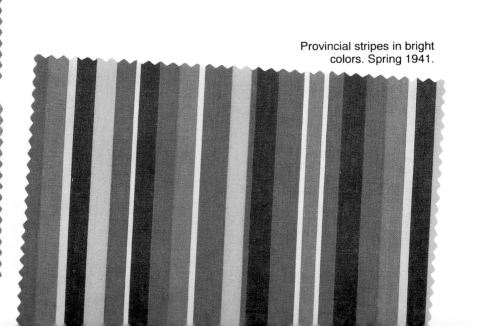

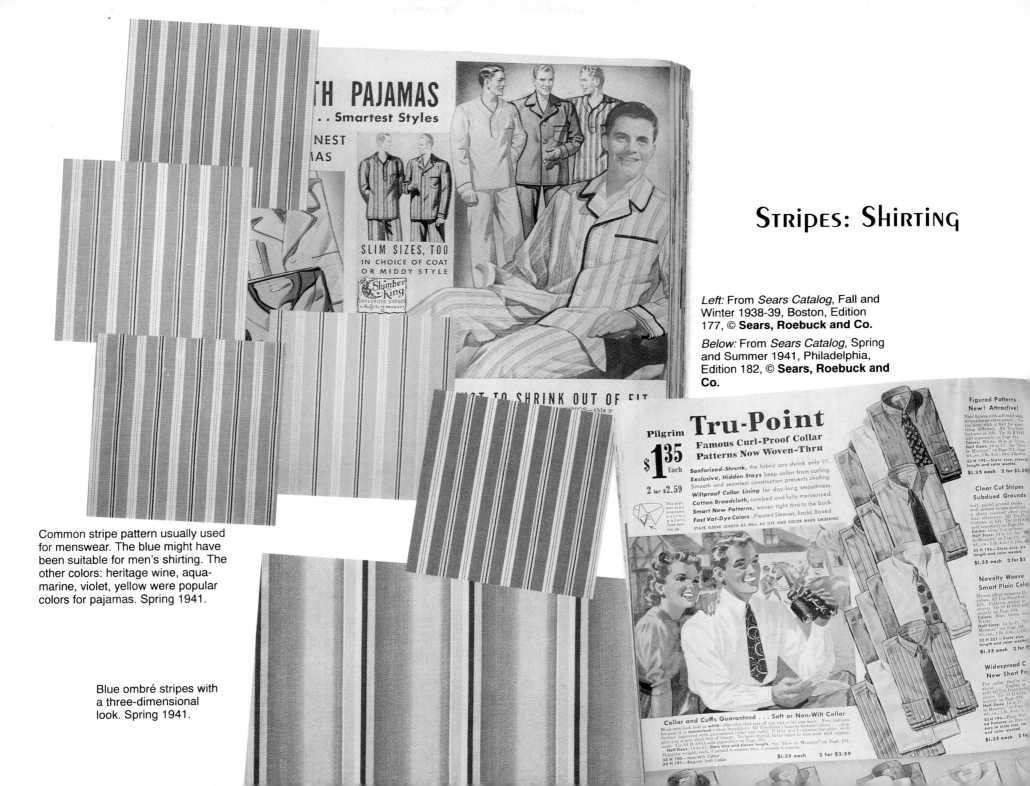

Stripes: Shirting

Left: From *Sears Catalog*, Fall and Winter 1938-39, Boston, Edition 177, © **Sears, Roebuck and Co.**

Below: From *Sears Catalog*, Spring and Summer 1941, Philadelphia, Edition 182, © **Sears, Roebuck and Co.**

Common stripe pattern usually used for menswear. The blue might have been suitable for men's shirting. The other colors: heritage wine, aquamarine, violet, yellow were popular colors for pajamas. Spring 1941.

Blue ombré stripes with a three-dimensional look. Spring 1941.

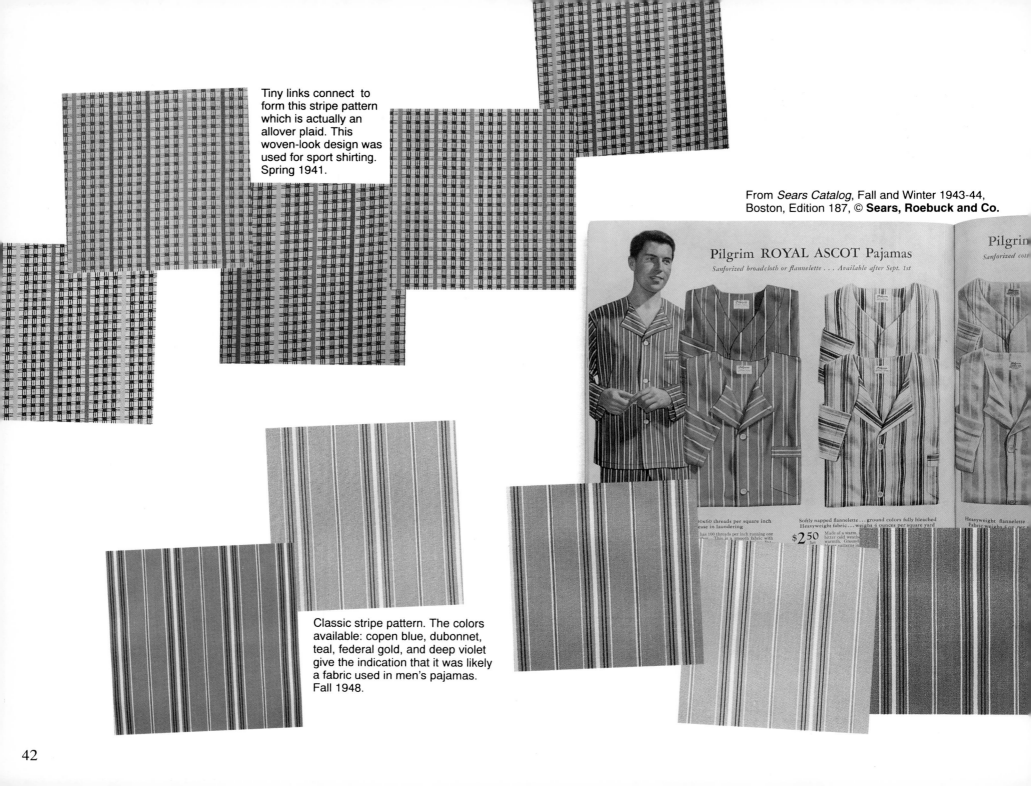

Tiny links connect to form this stripe pattern which is actually an allover plaid. This woven-look design was used for sport shirting. Spring 1941.

From *Sears Catalog*, Fall and Winter 1943-44, Boston, Edition 187, © **Sears, Roebuck and Co.**

Pilgrim ROYAL ASCOT Pajamas

Sanforized broadcloth or flannelette . . . Available after Sept. 1st

$2.50

Classic stripe pattern. The colors available: copen blue, dubonnet, teal, federal gold, and deep violet give the indication that it was likely a fabric used in men's pajamas. Fall 1948.

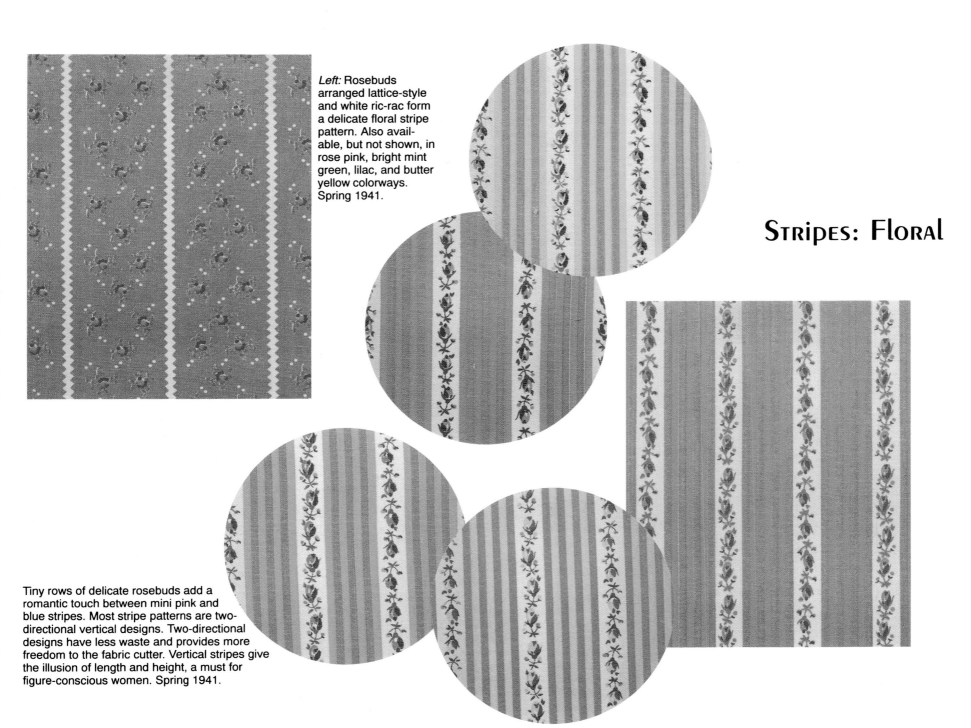

Left: Rosebuds arranged lattice-style and white ric-rac form a delicate floral stripe pattern. Also available, but not shown, in rose pink, bright mint green, lilac, and butter yellow colorways. Spring 1941.

Stripes: Floral

Tiny rows of delicate rosebuds add a romantic touch between mini pink and blue stripes. Most stripe patterns are two-directional vertical designs. Two-directional designs have less waste and provides more freedom to the fabric cutter. Vertical stripes give the illusion of length and height, a must for figure-conscious women. Spring 1941.

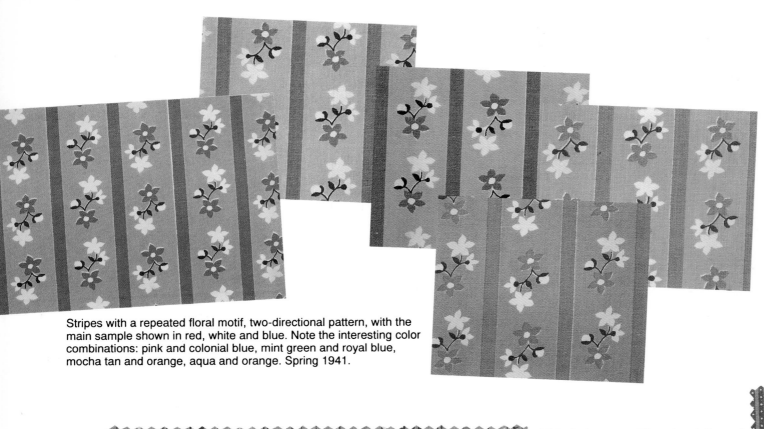

Stripes with a repeated floral motif, two-directional pattern, with the main sample shown in red, white and blue. Note the interesting color combinations: pink and colonial blue, mint green and royal blue, mocha tan and orange, aqua and orange. Spring 1941.

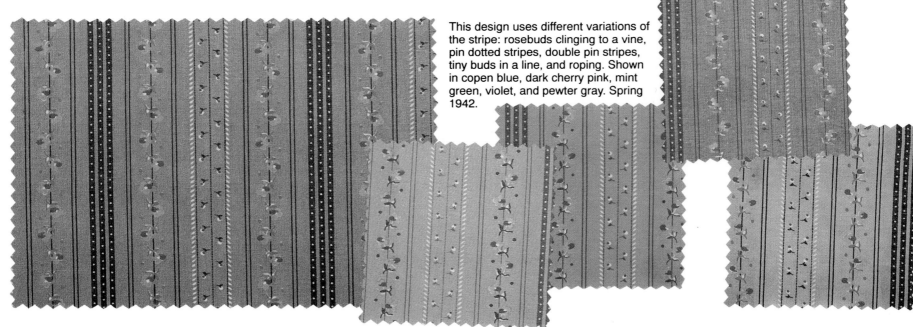

This design uses different variations of the stripe: rosebuds clinging to a vine, pin dotted stripes, double pin stripes, tiny buds in a line, and roping. Shown in copen blue, dark cherry pink, mint green, violet, and pewter gray. Spring 1942.

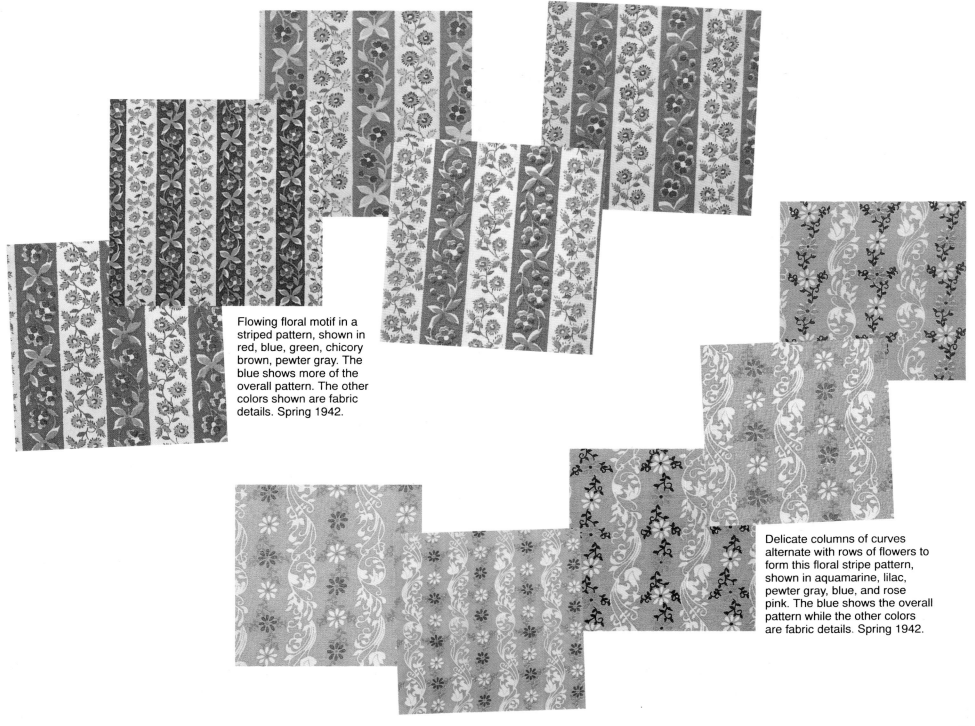

Flowing floral motif in a striped pattern, shown in red, blue, green, chicory brown, pewter gray. The blue shows more of the overall pattern. The other colors shown are fabric details. Spring 1942.

Delicate columns of curves alternate with rows of flowers to form this floral stripe pattern, shown in aquamarine, lilac, pewter gray, blue, and rose pink. The blue shows the overall pattern while the other colors are fabric details. Spring 1942.

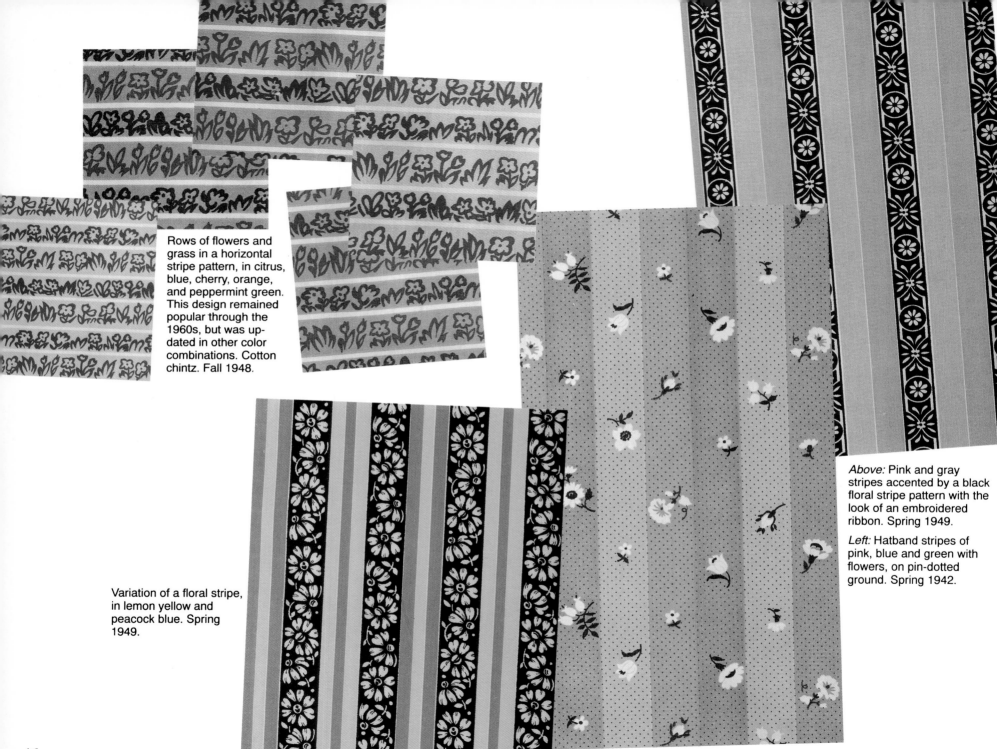

Rows of flowers and grass in a horizontal stripe pattern, in citrus, blue, cherry, orange, and peppermint green. This design remained popular through the 1960s, but was updated in other color combinations. Cotton chintz. Fall 1948.

Above: Pink and gray stripes accented by a black floral stripe pattern with the look of an embroidered ribbon. Spring 1949.

Left: Hatband stripes of pink, blue and green with flowers, on pin-dotted ground. Spring 1942.

Variation of a floral stripe, in lemon yellow and peacock blue. Spring 1949.

Yellow peonies and lacy diamonds create this bold stripe design. The positioning of the larger flowers would make this design a horizontal stripe pattern. This fabric probably would not have been used for dressmaking because most women find horizontal stripes to be unflattering for the figure. A likely use would be for making curtains. Shown also in pink. Fall 1948.

Stripes with a wide (actual size: 2-3/4" wide) lacy rose border, yellow and black horizontal stripe design, one-directional pattern. Other colors, not shown, royal blue/black, kelly green/black, red/black. Spring 1949.

47

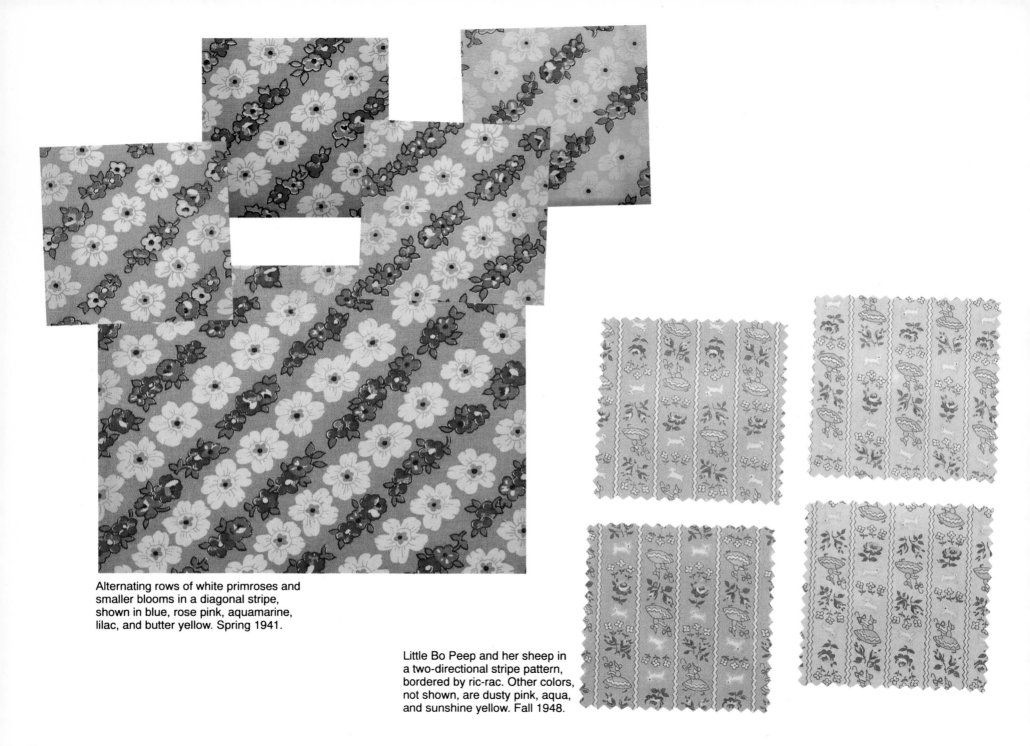

Alternating rows of white primroses and smaller blooms in a diagonal stripe, shown in blue, rose pink, aquamarine, lilac, and butter yellow. Spring 1941.

Little Bo Peep and her sheep in a two-directional stripe pattern, bordered by ric-rac. Other colors, not shown, are dusty pink, aqua, and sunshine yellow. Fall 1948.

STRIPES: FLORAL ON STRIPE

Colorful flowers on spaced pin stripe ground, in horizon blue, Miami rose, aquamarine, rust and royal blue. Spring 1942.

Peony clusters on a navy pin stripe ground, in another red, white and blue design. Other colors shown are bright red, copen blue, chocolate brown, charcoal gray. Spring 1941.

Flowers shadowed in black, on ticking stripe background. Cotton chintz. Spring 1949.

The unusual treatment of this stripe pattern uses dotted lines to simulate stitching. The predominant look of this design is neither a floral nor a stripe, but a combination of both. Spring 1941.

This spaced geometric combines hatband stripes with alternating pin stripes, two-directional pattern. Shown in cadet blue and burgundy. Also available, not shown, in dark cherry pink, navy, and nickel gray. Spring 1941.

This hatband stripe pattern combines many other design elements: a lattice ground, a repeated floral-like motif on the latticework, and florals with flowing stems that gives the design movement. Spring 1941.

Tiny flower clusters and pussywillow on diagonal stripes. The use of darker lines in the stripes lends depth by giving the design a raised, three-dimensional effect. Spring 1942.

Medium large flowers with blue shadows in an overall striped pattern. The speckled effect is a subtle way to suggest stripes, and gives the design a slightly textured look. Shown in concord blue, cherry pink, deep aquamarine, lilac, and butter yellow. Spring 1942.

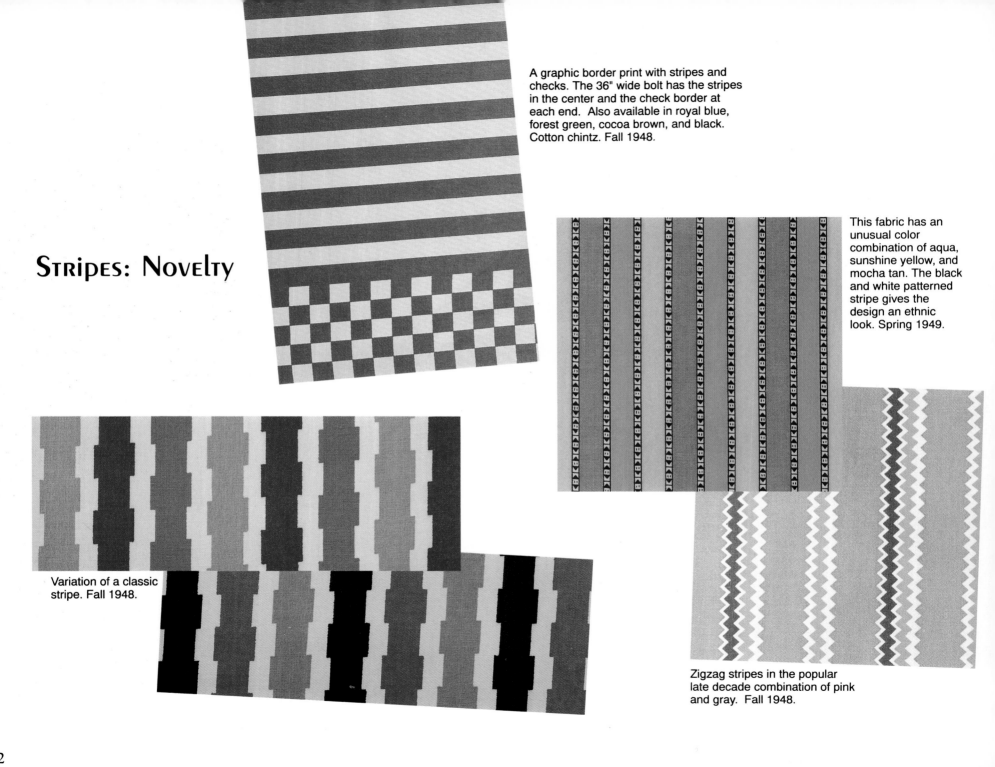

Stripes: Novelty

A graphic border print with stripes and checks. The 36" wide bolt has the stripes in the center and the check border at each end. Also available in royal blue, forest green, cocoa brown, and black. Cotton chintz. Fall 1948.

This fabric has an unusual color combination of aqua, sunshine yellow, and mocha tan. The black and white patterned stripe gives the design an ethnic look. Spring 1949.

Variation of a classic stripe. Fall 1948.

Zigzag stripes in the popular late decade combination of pink and gray. Fall 1948.

A feathery stripe pattern in pastel shades provides a soft background for the bold fretwork. In four color combinations. Spring 1949.

Brushstroke outline images of grapes on varied width wavy stripe pattern. Spring 1949.

53

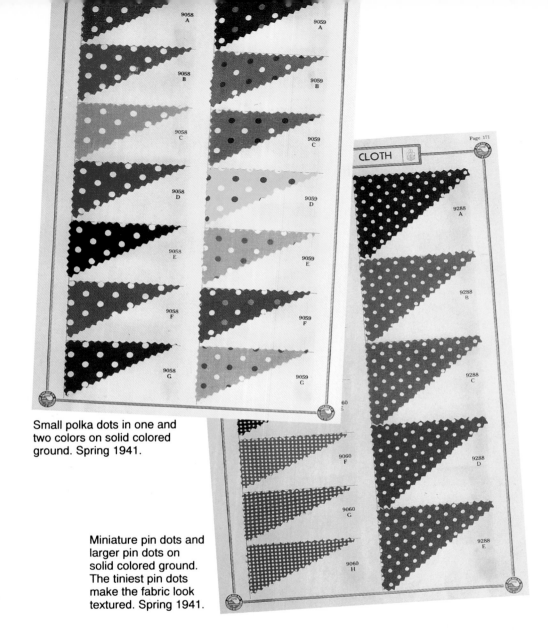

Small polka dots in one and two colors on solid colored ground. Spring 1941.

Miniature pin dots and larger pin dots on solid colored ground. The tiniest pin dots make the fabric look textured. Spring 1941.

Inset: The timeless polka-dot. These are about 5/8" in diameter actual size, a little smaller size than "coin dots". In blue and red. Spring 1941.

Right: From *Sears Catalog*, Spring and Summer 1941, Philadelphia, Edition 182, © **Sears, Roebuck and Co.**

DOTS: POLKA-DOTS

Dots: With Other Motifs

This variation of a polka-dot pattern cleverly uses concentric circles to create a new look. Closer examination will reveal an orderly design using equally spaced flowers. In copen blue, valley rose, aquamarine, lilac, and mocha tan. Spring 1942.

A wide daisy border (actual size: 4-1/2" wide) repeated every 8", runs vertically on a polka-dot ground. In the 36" wide bolt, the border repeats three times. Spring 1949.

Poppies and dots combine in a novelty print. Note the addition of black pin dots randomly tossed into the design. Spring 1949.

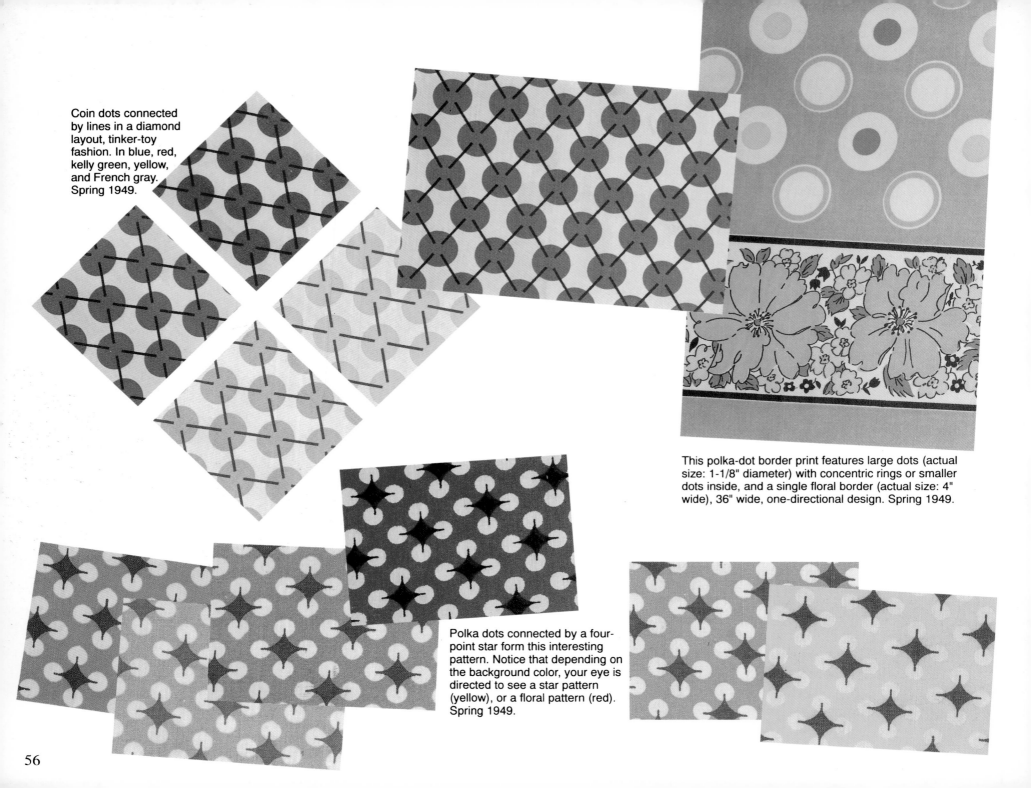

Coin dots connected by lines in a diamond layout, tinker-toy fashion. In blue, red, kelly green, yellow, and French gray. Spring 1949.

This polka-dot border print features large dots (actual size: 1-1/8" diameter) with concentric rings or smaller dots inside, and a single floral border (actual size: 4" wide), 36" wide, one-directional design. Spring 1949.

Polka dots connected by a four-point star form this interesting pattern. Notice that depending on the background color, your eye is directed to see a star pattern (yellow), or a floral pattern (red). Spring 1949.

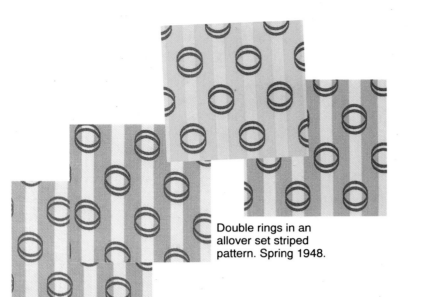

Double rings in an allover set striped pattern. Spring 1948.

Right: This pattern combines concentric circles and stripes. The placement of the stripes and circles gives this design a serpentine flow. Spring 1949.

Top: Concentric circles suggesting checkers pieces line up in a novelty stripe pattern. Spring 1949.

Dots and stripes combine in a unique pattern. The three connected dots could be seen as a molecular design, or is it a cartoon mouse? Spring 1949.

Double lines cross each dot in this interesting variation of a screw-top pattern that almost looks like baseballs. Available, not shown, in pink, aqua, navy, and maroon. Spring 1949.

From *Sears Catalog*, Fall and Winter 1938-39, Boston, Edition 177, © **Sears, Roebuck and Co.**

57

Variations of motifs in picotage, or "pinning" effect, give a block-print or relief look to the fabric. Spring 1941.

DoTS: Picotage Ground

9596
A

9596
B

9596
C

9596
D

9596
E

Flowers and leaves in a block-print look, using pinning as a design technique. Spring 1942.

The rose, the most popular flower in fabric design, is beautifully portrayed here on blue pin dot ground. Note the use of pinning to form the outline of tulips. Shown also in rose pink. Spring 1942.

Another variation of picotage or "pinning" technique in a floral design, creating a textured-look ground. Florals in red, blue, yellow, and green. Color not shown, purple flowers. Fall 1948.

Tiger lilies and daisies cover this bright spring chintz print, on pin dot ground. Cotton chintz. Also available, not shown, in pink, peacock blue, lemon yellow, and dawn gray. Spring 1949.

Floral. Sprigs of spring florals on tiny pin dot ground. Note the use of pinning as a shadow background for the flowers. Spring 1942.

Circles and Curves

Large asters on a ground of tiny French curves, allover print, on popular copen blue ground. Shown also in rose pink, and deep aquamarine. Also available, not shown, in lilac. Butter yellow is shown on the front cover. Spring 1941.

Variation of the French curves and floral theme. The addition of pin dots along the curves adds interest to the design. Fall 1948.

Variation of the same theme. Graceful curves lend movement to this design. Fall 1948.

Sweet floral wreaths in an overall spaced pattern, on white. Spring 1949.

From *Sears Catalog*, Spring and Summer 1941, Philadelphia, Edition 182, © **Sears, Roebuck and Co.**

Allover set design with a floral pinwheel motif. Cotton chintz. Spring 1949.

61

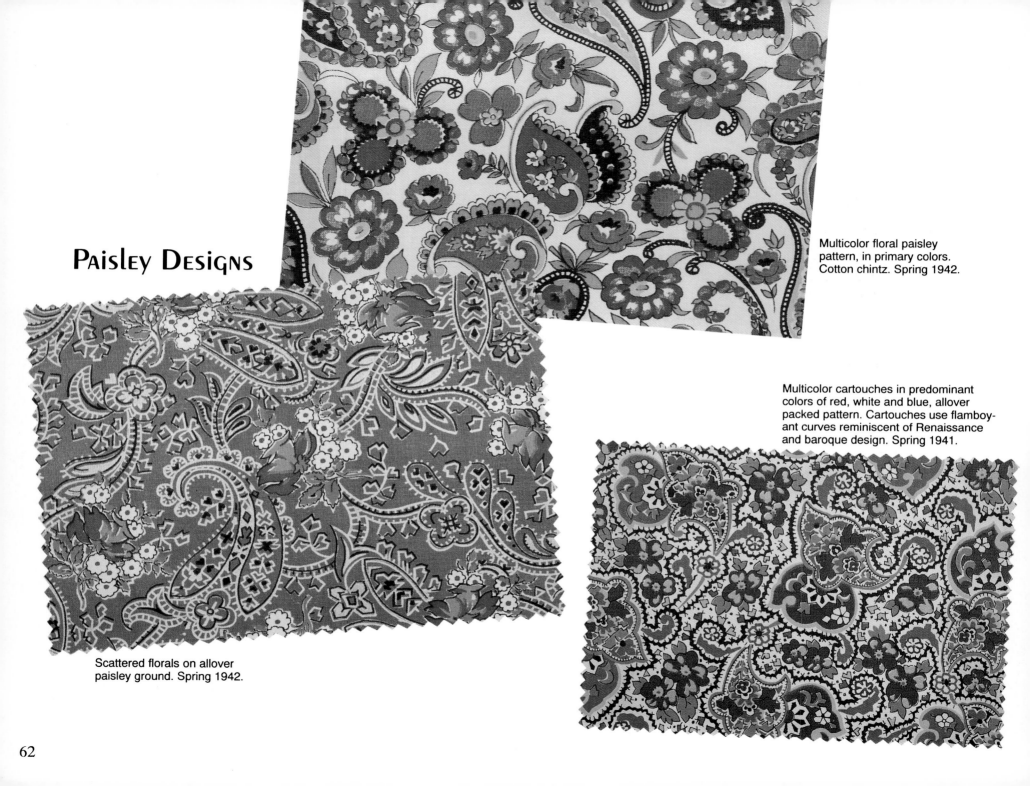

Paisley Designs

Multicolor floral paisley pattern, in primary colors. Cotton chintz. Spring 1942.

Multicolor cartouches in predominant colors of red, white and blue, allover packed pattern. Cartouches use flamboyant curves reminiscent of Renaissance and baroque design. Spring 1941.

Scattered florals on allover paisley ground. Spring 1942.

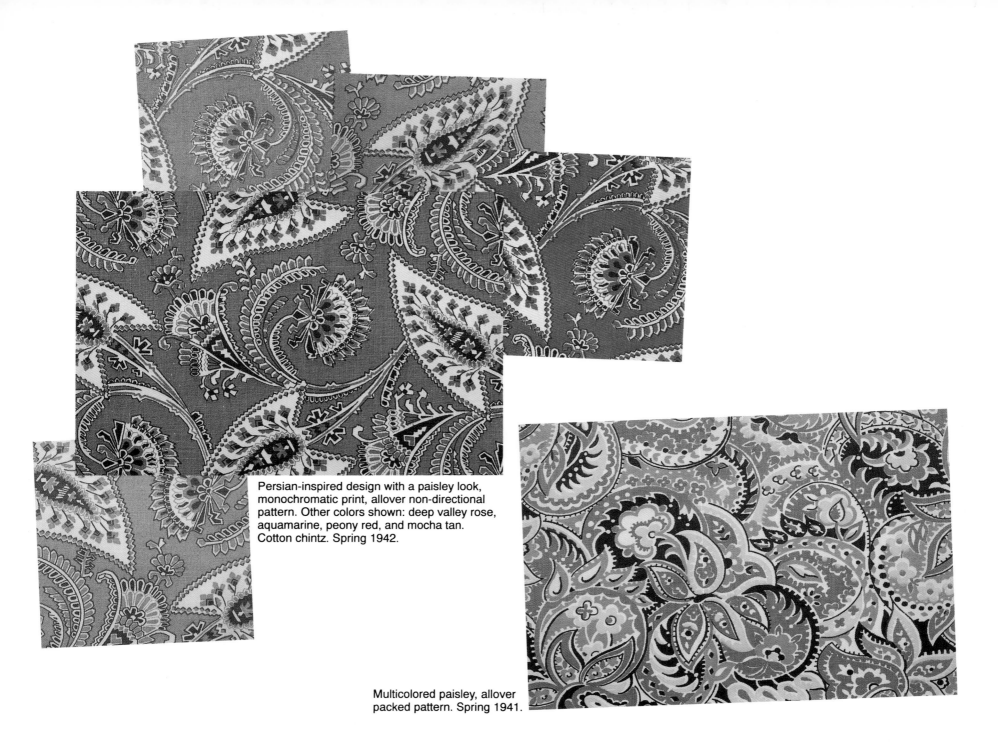

Persian-inspired design with a paisley look, monochromatic print, allover non-directional pattern. Other colors shown: deep valley rose, aquamarine, peony red, and mocha tan. Cotton chintz. Spring 1942.

Multicolored paisley, allover packed pattern. Spring 1941.

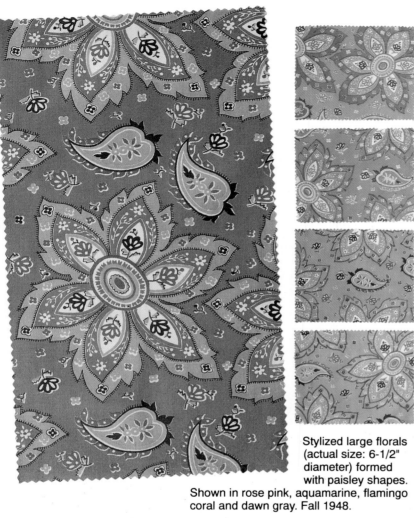

Stylized large florals
(actual size: 6-1/2"
diameter) formed
with paisley shapes.
Shown in rose pink, aquamarine, flamingo
coral and dawn gray. Fall 1948.

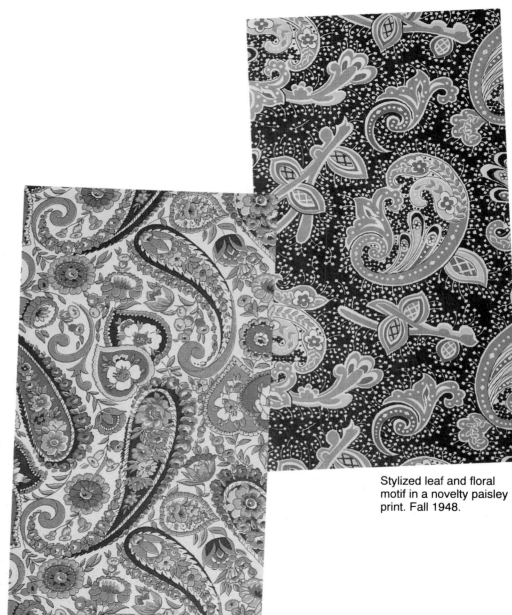

Stylized leaf and floral
motif in a novelty paisley
print. Fall 1948.

Hearts and flowers in a multicolor
floral paisley pattern. Spring 1949.

Butterflies flutter among stylized leaves in a beautiful multicolor paisley print. Note how well the butterfly wings match the paisley shapes. A great design! Spring 1949.

Very large and busy paisley design, in predominant colors of red, white, and blue, allover packed pattern. Spring 1941.

Very large fan-shaped paisley patterns (actual size: 7" spread). Cotton chintz. Fall 1948.

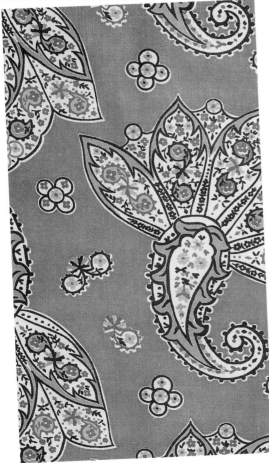

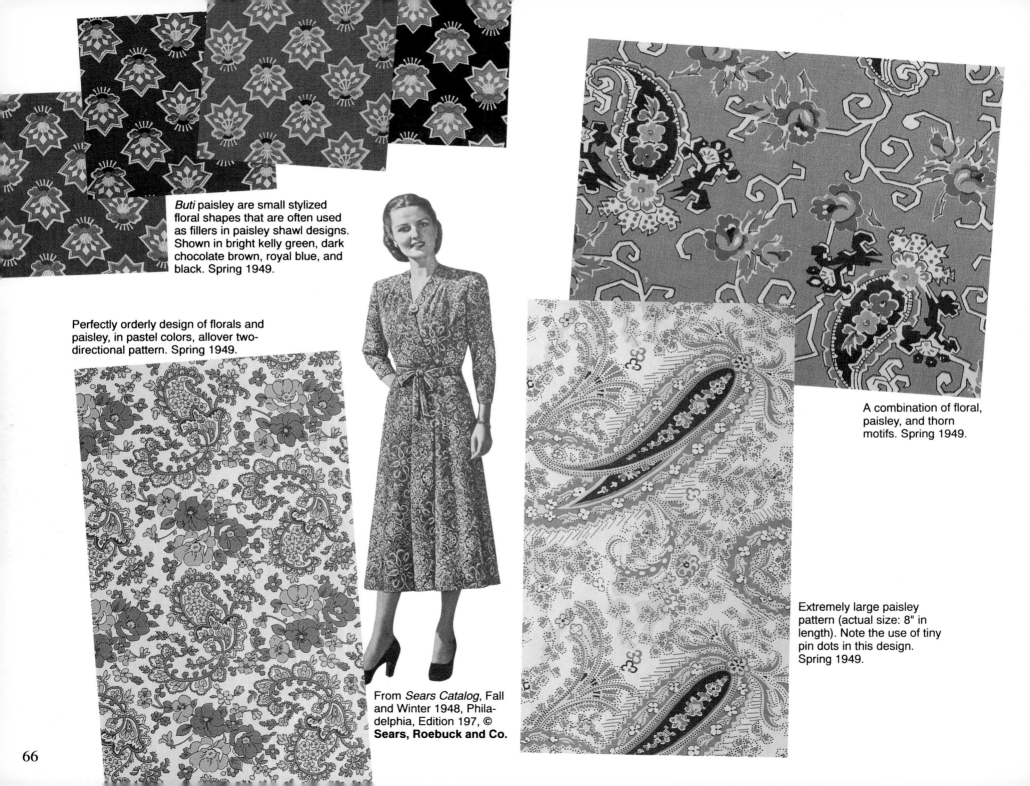

Buti paisley are small stylized floral shapes that are often used as fillers in paisley shawl designs. Shown in bright kelly green, dark chocolate brown, royal blue, and black. Spring 1949.

Perfectly orderly design of florals and paisley, in pastel colors, allover two-directional pattern. Spring 1949.

A combination of floral, paisley, and thorn motifs. Spring 1949.

From *Sears Catalog*, Fall and Winter 1948, Philadelphia, Edition 197, © **Sears, Roebuck and Co.**

Extremely large paisley pattern (actual size: 8" in length). Note the use of tiny pin dots in this design. Spring 1949.

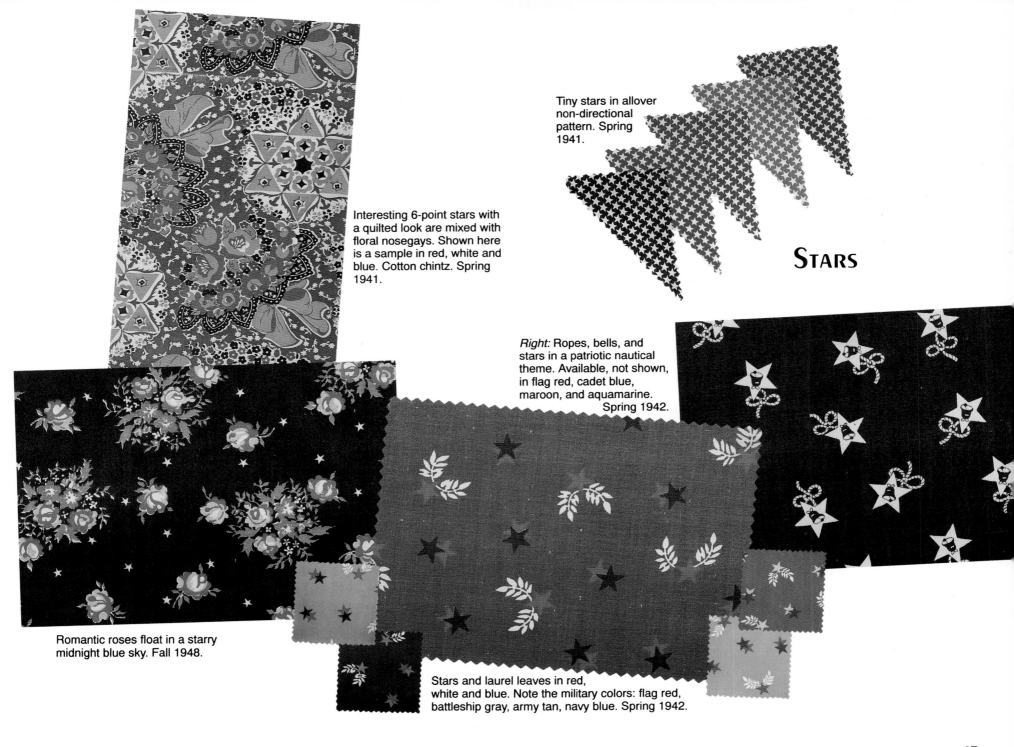

Interesting 6-point stars with a quilted look are mixed with floral nosegays. Shown here is a sample in red, white and blue. Cotton chintz. Spring 1941.

Tiny stars in allover non-directional pattern. Spring 1941.

STARS

Right: Ropes, bells, and stars in a patriotic nautical theme. Available, not shown, in flag red, cadet blue, maroon, and aquamarine. Spring 1942.

Romantic roses float in a starry midnight blue sky. Fall 1948.

Stars and laurel leaves in red, white and blue. Note the military colors: flag red, battleship gray, army tan, navy blue. Spring 1942.

Geometric Mix

Multiple motifs are evident in this design: floral, shooting stars, dots, stripes, checks and French curves. The layered design is not quite a quilted pattern but gives it the same overall look. Spring 1941.

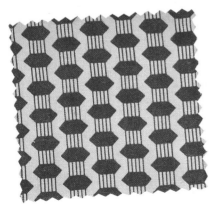

Pinstripes and hexagons. Cotton chintz. Spring 1949.

Squares and hexagons in an allover set pattern. Fall 1948.

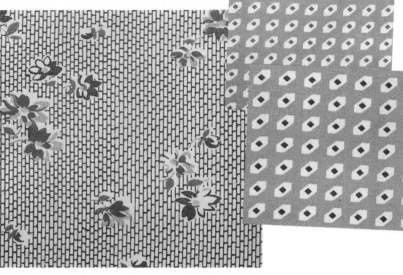

Florals on spaced geometric ground. The tiny rectangles laid out in a brick-like pattern give the fabric a textured woven effect. Also available, not shown, in colors of rose, violet, sage green, and navy blue. Spring 1941.

Tangerine florals and chartreuse leaves combine with a cellular honeycomb motif in a spaced abstract design. The interest in post-war science and technology popularized cellular and other abstract shapes as design motifs starting in the late 1940s and continuing into the first half of the 1950s. Fall 1948.

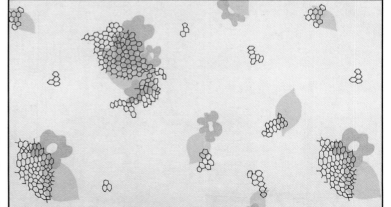

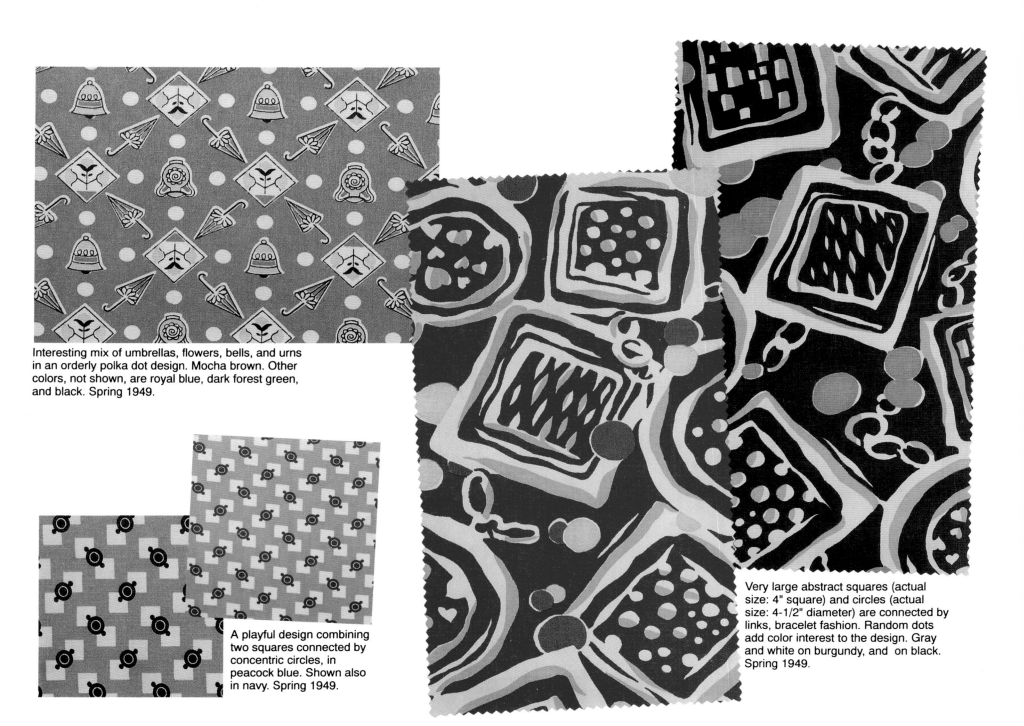

Interesting mix of umbrellas, flowers, bells, and urns in an orderly polka dot design. Mocha brown. Other colors, not shown, are royal blue, dark forest green, and black. Spring 1949.

A playful design combining two squares connected by concentric circles, in peacock blue. Shown also in navy. Spring 1949.

Very large abstract squares (actual size: 4" square) and circles (actual size: 4-1/2" diameter) are connected by links, bracelet fashion. Random dots add color interest to the design. Gray and white on burgundy, and on black. Spring 1949.

Floral Designs

Floral: Monotone Prints

Very large sunflowers (actual size: 5" diameter), narcissus, and oak leaves in a monotone print. This unique design uses positive and negative images of the motifs. Also available in valley rose, midnight blue, red, and cocoa brown. Cotton chintz. Fall 1948.

Large poppy-like anemones (actual size: 3"-3 1/2" spread), white on royal blue. Also available, not shown, in bright red, black, tea rose, and cocoa brown. Cotton chintz. Spring 1942.

Very large graphic interpretation of leaves and flowers (actual size: 8" spread), on navy ground. Other colors, not shown, cadet blue, flag red, horizon blue, cocoa brown. Cotton chintz. Spring 1942.

Very large graphic interpretation of florals (actual size 9" diameter), monotone patio print, allover packed pattern. Also available, not shown, in red, sage green, sunshine yellow, and black. Cotton chintz. Spring 1942.

Large graphic interpretation of daisies (actual size: 6 1/2" diameter), navy on white ground, allover packed design. Also available, not shown, in glory red, aircorps blue, Burmuda blue, and chicory brown. Cotton chintz. Spring 1942.

Advertisement to show wearability and the "tubfast," "sunfast" colors of Quadrica Cloth. 1947.

71

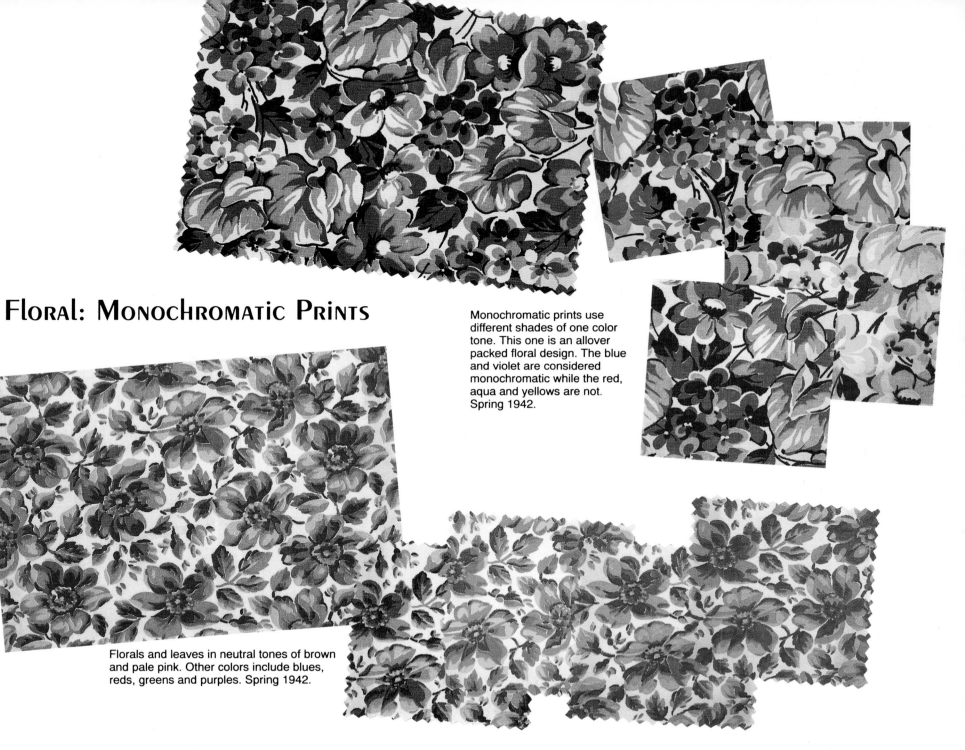

Floral: Monochromatic Prints

Monochromatic prints use different shades of one color tone. This one is an allover packed floral design. The blue and violet are considered monochromatic while the red, aqua and yellows are not. Spring 1942.

Florals and leaves in neutral tones of brown and pale pink. Other colors include blues, reds, greens and purples. Spring 1942.

Large cabbage roses (actual size: 5"
spread) and tulips, monochromatic print
in blue, red, aquamarine, and violet. The
gray swatch with an added touch of red
is not considered a monochromatic print.
Cotton chintz. Fall 1948.

Floral: Two-tone Prints

Branches of forsythia blooms, monotone print, on copen blue ground. Other colors: rose pink, aquamarine, lilac, and butter yellow. This design has a tropical feel. Spring 1941.

Stylized peonies on copen blue ground. Also available, not shown: in pink, aqua, desert sand, silver gray. Fall 1948.

Navy blue floral, allover tossed design, on copen blue ground. Other colors: dark wine on rose pink, navy on aquamarine, deep violet on lilac, chocolate brown on bright yellow. Spring 1941.

Floral: Mother and Daughter Prints

Mother and Daughter patterns provide a fashion alternative for the 1940s seamstress. The fabric design and colors are similar, however, the design motif is significantly reduced in size to accommodate the child. In this pattern, florals in the shape of butterflies flutter on a horizon blue field of white raindrops. Spring 1941.

From *Sears Catalog*, Spring and Summer 1945, Boston, Edition 190, © **Sears, Roebuck and Co.**

Floral: Twin Prints

A *twin print* uses the same pattern and colors in a coordinating, yet contrasting, fabric. *Above:* The gray in the first fabric is used as a shadow outline in the twin print with navy blue background. *Below left:* The yellow ground of the first print is used as a shadow outline in its twin print in chocolate brown. Spring 1941.

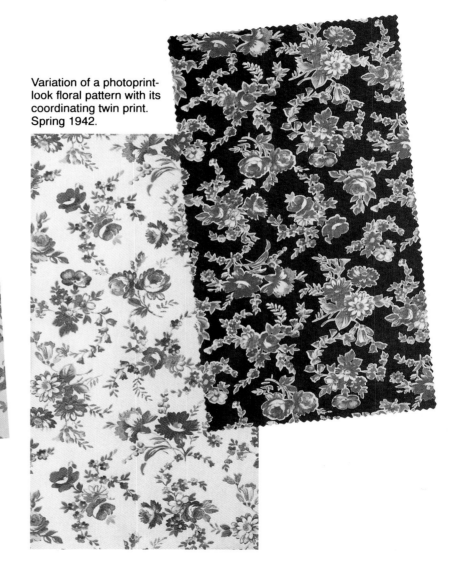

Variation of a photoprint-look floral pattern with its coordinating twin print. Spring 1942.

Scattered florals on aquamarine background. Twin print in teal.

Left: A spring print with colorful tulips on a patterned floral ground of dogwood blossoms, allover packed design. Note the pinning on the tiny background flowers. This print continued to sell until the end of the decade. Spring 1942.

Floral: Allover Packed Designs

Allover packed designs feature more design than background. *Right*: Tiny roses and leaves in an allover packed pattern. Notice that each flower and leaf branch is completely separated from the others, leaving a consistent dark navy ground around each object. Fall 1948.

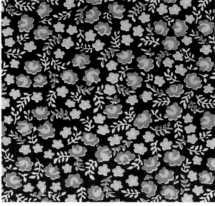

The green in this daisy floral pattern gives a bright contrast against the navy ground. Allover non-directional print. Fall 1948.

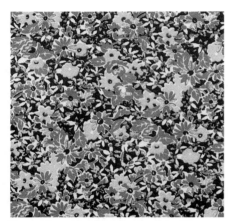

Busy allover packed floral print with bright red and yellow flowers. Note the use of picotage in the background flowers. Fall 1948.

Dianthus, a type of carnation, in an allover packed pattern. Spring 1949.

Pink and blue poppy mallows, allover packed pattern. Spring 1941.

Left: Daisies, asters, and violets in an allover packed design. Coral and violet makes for an interesting color combination. Spring 1949.

Right: Clusters of red and blue roses, allover non-directional pattern. Spring 1941.

Daisies and anemones in an allover packed design, two-directional pattern, shown in blue, cherry red and violet. Spring 1941.

Packed cloth sale at a Washington, D.C. department store. 1947.

Floral: Allover-Tossed Designs

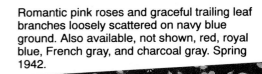

Romantic pink roses and graceful trailing leaf branches loosely scattered on navy blue ground. Also available, not shown, red, royal blue, French gray, and charcoal gray. Spring 1942.

Allover tossed designs are closely packed designs with a non-directional pattern. In floral designs, flowers and leaves are usually tossed in random fashion, with stems and branches pointing in different directions. *Above:* Miniature white flowers and flowing leaf branches scatter on a bright copen blue ground. Available in four additional colorways: rose pink, mint green, lilac, and butter yellow. Spring 1941.

Left: Repeated from the previous year, this design was printed in darker colors. Shown in navy, cranberry, chicory brown, violet, and charcoal gray. Spring 1942.

Right: Roses in an allover tossed print. Note the graceful curves of the stems in the design. Other colors, not shown, in cherry pink, lilac, sunshine yellow, and turquoise. Fall 1948.

Tiny floral print in an allover tossed, non-directional pattern. The design is complimented by black and white "S" strokes and pin dots. Fall 1948.

Tiny clusters of violets, allover tossed, non-directional print. Also available with pink, lilac, yellow, gray flowers. Spring 1941.

Right: This freesia print effectively uses dark wine red to contrast the subtle blues, and bright cactus green to contrast the kelly green in the leaves. Not shown: with freesias in muted shades of peach, lilac, mustard yellow, and gray. Spring 1941.

Allover print of red and blue florals on white ground. The use of gray as a "shadow" image of the design gives the fabric a full but less cluttered look. Spring 1942.

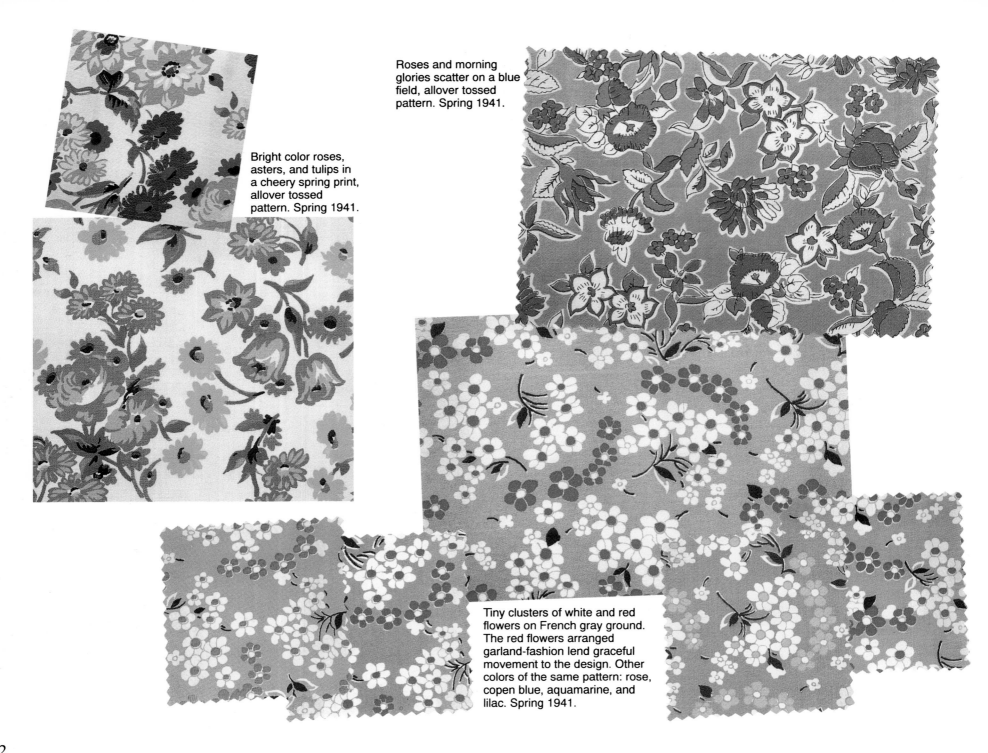

Bright color roses, asters, and tulips in a cheery spring print, allover tossed pattern. Spring 1941.

Roses and morning glories scatter on a blue field, allover tossed pattern. Spring 1941.

Tiny clusters of white and red flowers on French gray ground. The red flowers arranged garland-fashion lend graceful movement to the design. Other colors of the same pattern: rose, copen blue, aquamarine, and lilac. Spring 1941.

Right: Clusters of violets in another red, white and blue design. Spring 1942.

Below: Roses and carnations in an allover non-directional pattern. The pale blue carnations against the bright red roses gives the design a less-packed look. Spring 1949.

Below: Splashy red tulips and lilacs in an allover packed pattern. Spring 1949.

Above: Sprigs of rosebuds in a scattered print, on bright copen blue ground. Other colorways, not shown, in cherry pink, aqua, lilac, and sunshine yellow. Fall 1948.

83

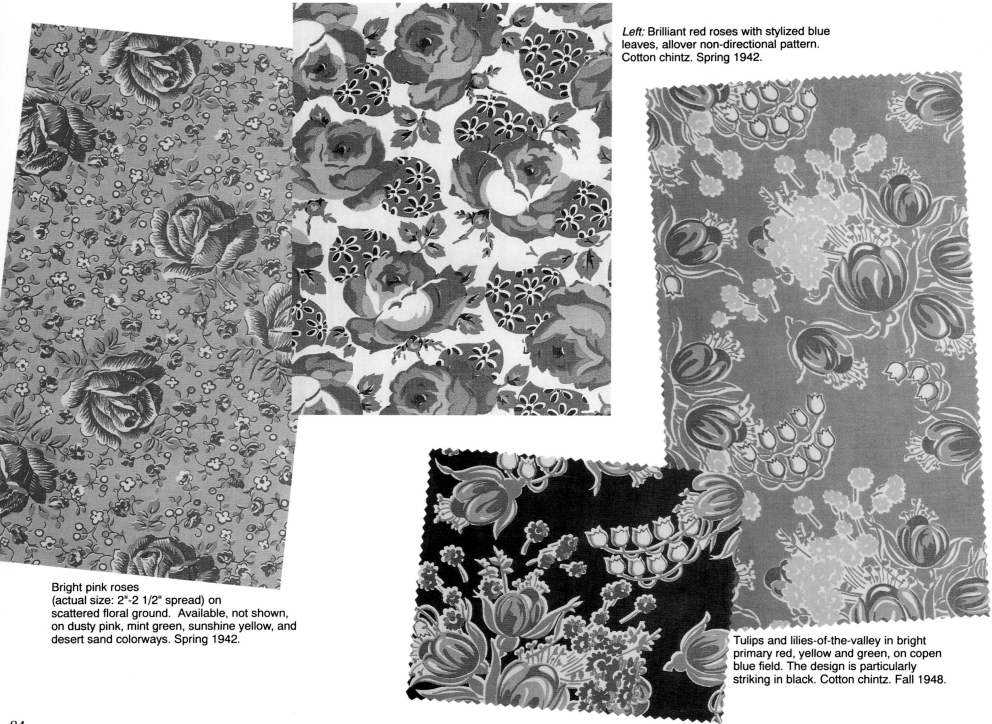

Left: Brilliant red roses with stylized blue leaves, allover non-directional pattern. Cotton chintz. Spring 1942.

Bright pink roses
(actual size: 2"-2 1/2" spread) on scattered floral ground. Available, not shown, on dusty pink, mint green, sunshine yellow, and desert sand colorways. Spring 1942.

Tulips and lilies-of-the-valley in bright primary red, yellow and green, on copen blue field. The design is particularly striking in black. Cotton chintz. Fall 1948.

Magnolia and cherry blossoms in a dramatic print. Shown in copen blue, cherry pink, mint green, nickel gray, and deep aquamarine. Spring 1942.

The ever popular poppy and tulips presented in bright, spashy reds and greens, on horizon blue ground. Shown also in butter yellow. The use of shading in the flowers lend depth to the design. Spring 1942.

Poppies and other flowers
loosely scattered on white
ground. An eye-catching
print for Spring. 1941.

From *Sears Catalog*,
Spring and Summer 1945,
Boston, Edition 190, ©
Sears, Roebuck and Co.

Anemones, a popular poppy-like flower,
were often used in fabric designs during
this period. Here is another interpretation,
with graceful curling stems in popular
copen blue. Also shown in rose pink and
deep aquamarine. Spring 1941.

Floral: Spaced, Non-Directional

A *spaced* design has equal or more background as compared with the design motif. This non-directional pattern features scattered daisies in a copen blue field. Other dramatic colors include red, midnight blue, and yellow. Colors not shown include dawn gray, aquamarine, mocha tan, and black. Fall 1948.

Far right: Strong, well-defined design of red poppies and white daisies on a field of bright copen blue, non-directional pattern. Spring 1941.

Near right: Colorful clematis in a field of blue, non-directional pattern. Also available in French gray, cherry pink, aqua, desert sand and sunshine yellow. Fall 1948.

Very large peonies
(actual sizes: 4-1/2" -
6-1/2" diameter).
Variations of this design
appeared well into the
1950s. Shown: red florals
on copen blue, and royal
blue florals on red. Cotton
chintz. Fall 1948.

Right: Very large red
peonies on white,
non-directional
pattern. Cotton
chintz. Spring 1942.

From *Sears Catalog*, Fall
and Winter 1943-44, Boston,
Edition 187, © **Sears,
Roebuck and Co.**

Left: Very large poppies (actual sizes: 4"-6" spread) on horizon blue. This design is fairly simple but the size and colors offer a dramatic impact. Shown also, from left to right: in rose pink, glory blue, sunlight yellow, black, and chestnut brown. Cotton chintz. Spring 1942.

Peonies (actual size: 7-1/2" diameter) in a very bold floral print, on navy blue, French gray, and dark charcoal ground. Cotton chintz. Fall 1948.

Floral: Two-Directional

Right: Sprigs of white blooms accented by red. Large two-directional print featuring patriotic colors appropriate for the times. Spring 1941.

The orderly large red and tiny white florals at first glance look like a loosely scattered pattern, on copen blue two-directional print. Also shown in rose, aquamarine, lilac, and butter yellow. Spring 1941.

A floral design in red, white and blue, allover two-directional pattern. Also shown in wine red, and black. Spring 1942.

Another interpretation of poppies
(actual size: 2-1/2" diameter) and
daisies. Spring 1942.

Above: Variation of a spring bouquet,
on dark blue ground. Spring 1942.

Left: Large sprays of poppies, daisies,
and asters with dawn gray shadow
effect, in bright primary colors on white
ground. Spring 1942.

Floral: Photoprints

Above: Photoprint of very large poppies (actual size 5"-5 1/2" in diameter), allover non-directional design. Cotton chintz. Spring 1942.

Above: Spectacular tiger lilies and other garden flowers (actual size: 5" diameter), allover non-directional photoprint. Cotton chintz. Fall 1948.

Left: Multicolor sprays of spring flowers, with red as the predominant color, two-directional photoprint. Spring 1941.

Right: Beautiful roses (actual size: 5" spread) and hydrangea, multi-colored photoprint. Cotton chintz. Fall 1948.

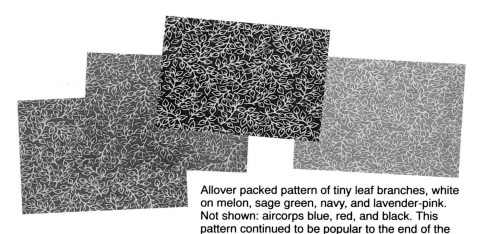

Floral: Leaves

Allover packed pattern of tiny leaf branches, white on melon, sage green, navy, and lavender-pink. Not shown: aircorps blue, red, and black. This pattern continued to be popular to the end of the decade, and without color changes. Spring 1942.

Right: The graphic images of leaves in this design have a light and airy feel. Available, not shown, in rose pink, aquamarine, lilac, and sunshine yellow. Spring 1942.

Leaves arranged in a random snowflake pattern, white and navy on colonial blue, and butter yellow. Available, not shown, in rose pink, peacock blue, and nickel gray. Spring 1942.

From *Sears Catalog*, Spring and Summer 1941, Philadelphia, Edition 182, © **Sears, Roebuck and Co.**

The graceful curves of a leaf branch are the dominant theme in this floral design, on colonial blue ground, allover non-directional pattern. Shown also in cherry pink and lilac. Spring 1941.

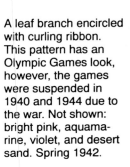

A leaf branch encircled with curling ribbon. This pattern has an Olympic Games look, however, the games were suspended in 1940 and 1944 due to the war. Not shown: bright pink, aquamarine, violet, and desert sand. Spring 1942.

Splashy patio print with a tropical floral and leaf design, in rust brown and greens. Cotton chintz. Spring 1941.

Large graphic image of a cactus bush with its outstretched leaves, or "spines" (actual size: 6" spread), in red, white and blue, non-directional pattern. Cotton chintz. Spring 1942.

Floral: Whimsical Interpretation

Sprays of spring flowers on spaced blue ground, two-directional pattern. Spring 1941.

Stylized florals in red, white and blue theme, allover tossed pattern. Shown also in cherry pink. Spring 1941.

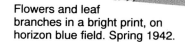

Flowers and leaf branches in a bright print, on horizon blue field. Spring 1942.

Roses framed in white lace medallions, allover non-directional pattern. Spring 1942.

Tiny print of rosebuds and lace, allover non-directional pattern. Spring 1942.

Jacobean-look floral print, allover non-directional pattern. Spring 1942.

The poppy is a recurring motif in floral fabric designs of the period. Here is an interesting variation of poppies and other flowers surrounded by white puffs. Spring 1942.

A single anemone framed by scallop edging adds a romantic look of lace to this pattern. Allover non-directional print. Fall 1948.

Whimsical treatment of daisies tied with pink bowknots, spaced layout on colonial blue ground, non-directional pattern. Spring 1941.

Left: Stylized florals and pagoda images in an allover non-directional pattern. Muslin. Fall 1948.

Beautiful graphic interpretation of the rose, shown here in red, yellow and blue. Spring 1941.

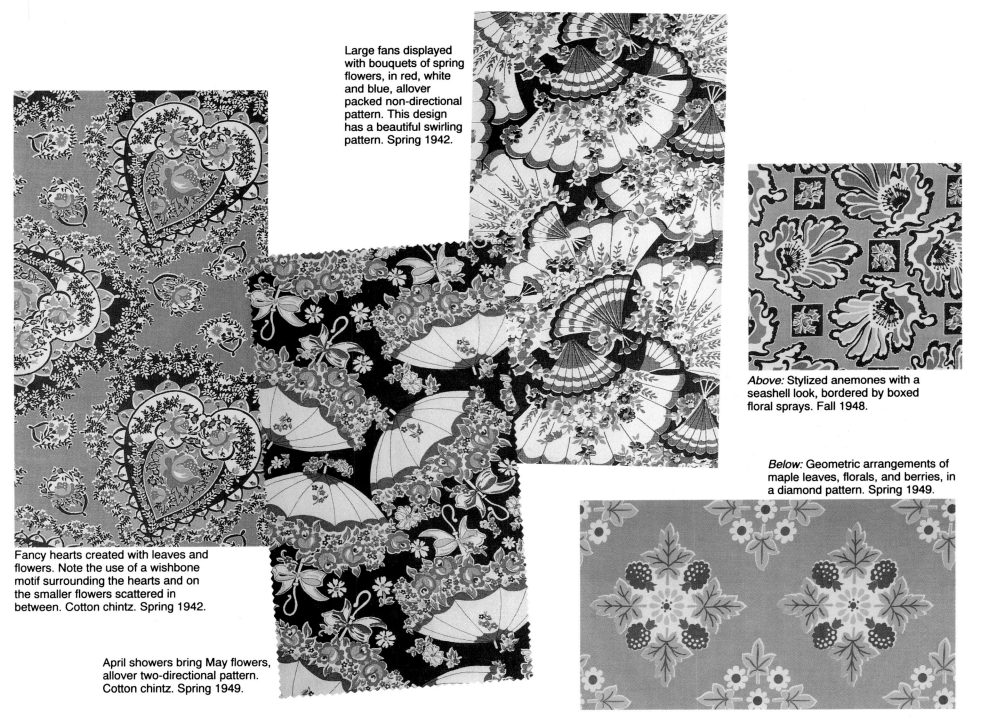

Large fans displayed with bouquets of spring flowers, in red, white and blue, allover packed non-directional pattern. This design has a beautiful swirling pattern. Spring 1942.

Above: Stylized anemones with a seashell look, bordered by boxed floral sprays. Fall 1948.

Below: Geometric arrangements of maple leaves, florals, and berries, in a diamond pattern. Spring 1949.

Fancy hearts created with leaves and flowers. Note the use of a wishbone motif surrounding the hearts and on the smaller flowers scattered in between. Cotton chintz. Spring 1942.

April showers bring May flowers, allover two-directional pattern. Cotton chintz. Spring 1949.

Novelty Designs

Novelty: Fruit Prints

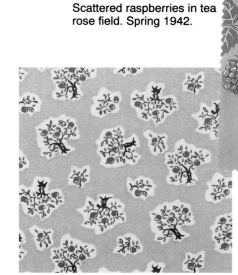

Scattered raspberries in tea rose field. Spring 1942.

Left: Apple trees and branches in blue. Also in pale pink, pale peacock blue, chartreuse, and dawn gray. Chartreuse is a color not seen in early decade design, but became, along with rose tones, a popular post-war choice. Spring 1949.

Strawberries and blossoms on horizon blue ground, allover non-directional pattern. Also shown: a "twin print" having reverse colors of blue blossoms on white ground. Spring 1942.

Strawberries cover a field of dogwood blossoms. Also available and not shown in pink, aquamarine, lemon yellow, and dawn gray. Cotton chintz. Spring 1949.

Even fruit comes in patriotic colors of red, white and blue.
This design features apples, grapes, raspberries, and
cherries in an overall non-directional pattern. Spring 1941.

Photoprint of fruit
including apples,
berries and grapes.
Cotton chintz.
Spring 1942.

© catalog p.854,
Fall and Winter
1948, Philadel-
phia, Edition
197, **Sears,
Roebuck and
Co.**

Large-scale photoprint
design with peaches,
cherries, and berries.
Cotton chintz. Fall 1948.

A Plastic top set $87.85

B Plastic top set $

Spring-filled seats

C Porcelain top set $64.85

Right: Homey country garden images in box layout. Tulips in a circular wreath pattern and ribbons surround each square. In red, white and blue cotton chintz. Spring 1941.

Below: Teacups, teapots, watering can, and a plate with utensils positioned like a clock, in large tile layout. Borders have tiny checks. Red was a popular choice for kitchens. Cotton chintz. Spring 1941.

Novelty: Kitchen Designs

Matched Towel and Toweling
"Garden Print" for brighter kitchens

39¢ each Towel   40¢ Toweling yard

Brilliant new striped Toweling 40¢ yard

Far left: Homey images arranged in a large windowbox check pattern, obviously meant for use in the kitchen as curtains or aprons. Note the clever use of eating utensils in the stripes. Primary colors. Cotton chintz. Spring 1941.

Left: From *Sears Catalog*, p.725, Fall and Winter 1943-44, Boston, Edition 187, © **Sears, Roebuck and Co.**

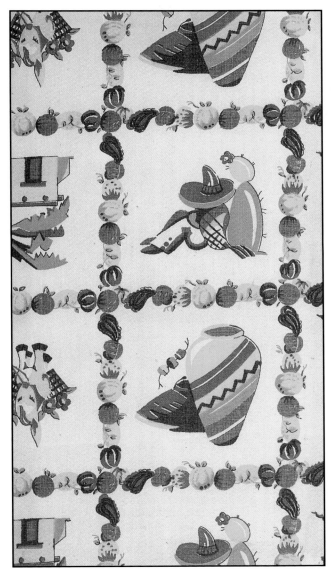

Mexican village theme print in large boxed layout, bordered in fruit and vegetables motif, primary colors. Muslin. Spring 1942.

Right: Mexican themed design in large boxed layout, bordered with multicolored stripes, buttons, and 8-point stars. Cotton chintz. Fall 1948.

Left: Mexican motif in large boxed layout, bordered in directional triangles. Spring 1941.

Novelty: Exotic Images

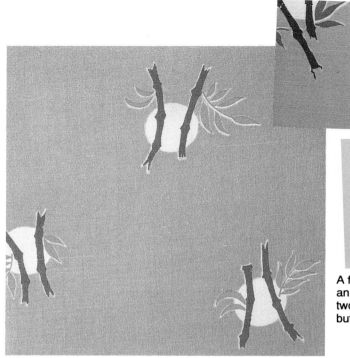

A full moon framed by bamboo gives this pattern an exotic feel, on spaced horizon blue ground, two-directional pattern. Also shown in aqua and butter yellow. Spring 1941.

Hawaiian hula girls and coconut palms. Fall 1948.

Grazing pandas and bamboo design, non-directional pattern, on khaki tan. Available, not shown, in concord blue, red, cadet blue, and slate gray. Fall 1948.

Novelty: People Images

Children at work and play in a country field, cadet blue ground, non-directional pattern. Spring 1941.

Little girls and teddy bears in a field of tiny red pin dots, non-directional pattern. Spring 1941.

A New York department store's cloth sale. 1946.

Above: A little boy and his kitten hard at work spring planting, allover non-directional pattern. Other colors, not shown, are pink, aqua, yellow and peach. Cotton chintz. Spring 1949.

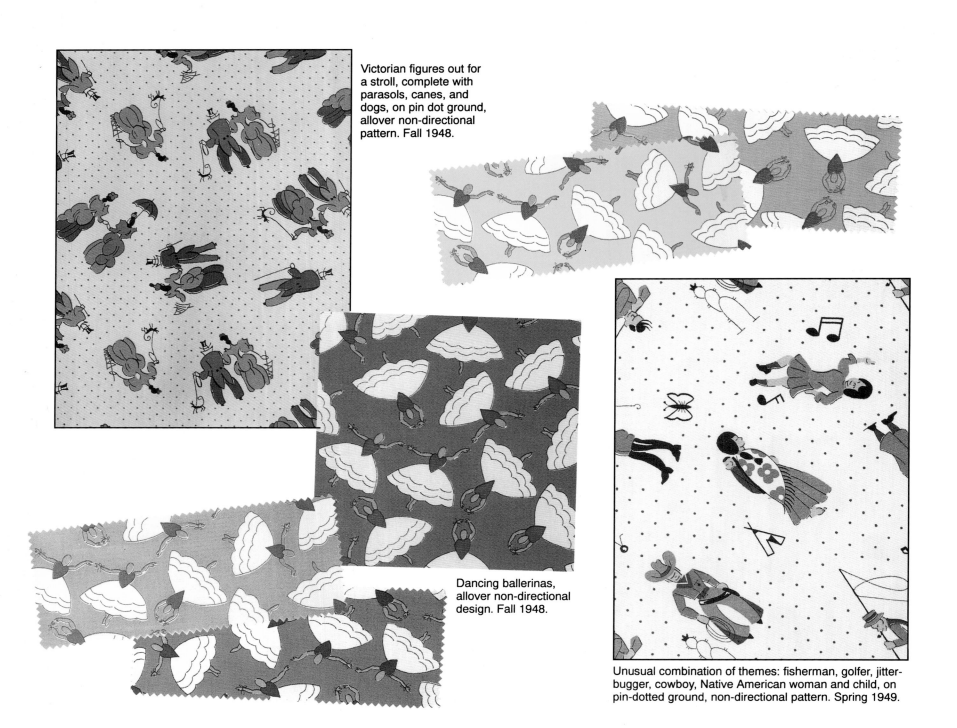

Victorian figures out for a stroll, complete with parasols, canes, and dogs, on pin dot ground, allover non-directional pattern. Fall 1948.

Dancing ballerinas, allover non-directional design. Fall 1948.

Unusual combination of themes: fisherman, golfer, jitter-bugger, cowboy, Native American woman and child, on pin-dotted ground, non-directional pattern. Spring 1949.

106

Bunny rabbits in a variety of poses, child's print. These colors were common for children: Cherry pink, mint green, pale peach, butter yellow. Spring 1941.

Novelty: Children's Designs

Children's pattern with squirrels, bears, bunnies and donkeys. Shown in blue, pale pink, aquamarine, melon, and sunshine yellow. Spring 1942.

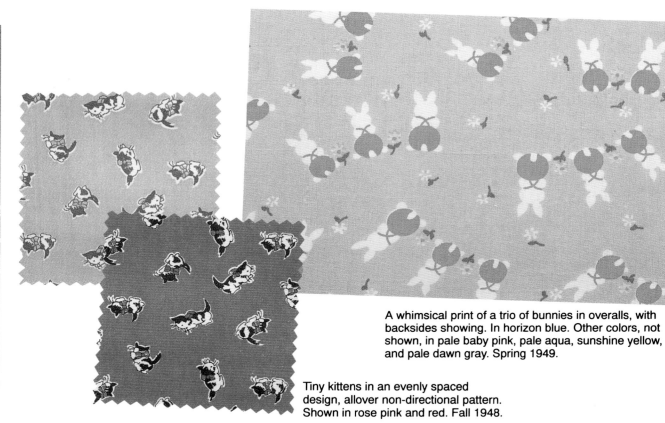

A whimsical print of a trio of bunnies in overalls, with backsides showing. In horizon blue. Other colors, not shown, in pale baby pink, pale aqua, sunshine yellow, and pale dawn gray. Spring 1949.

Tiny kittens in an evenly spaced design, allover non-directional pattern. Shown in rose pink and red. Fall 1948.

Large bunny rabbits (actual size: 5" high) in a variety of poses, at play and work. Also available, not shown, in cherry pink, aquamarine, heritage wine, and navy blue. Cotton chintz. Spring 1942.

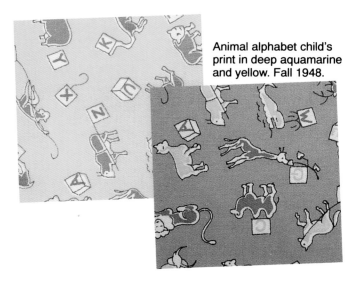

Animal alphabet child's print in deep aquamarine and yellow. Fall 1948.

Little chicks wearing a variety of hats, with an interesting pin dot background. Spring 1942.

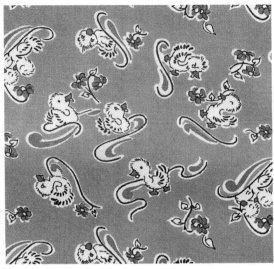

This children's print tells the story of the three little pigs and the big bad wolf. Fall 1948.

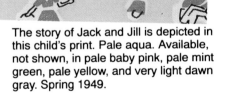

Ducklings frolicking in a pond. Other colors, not shown, in this pattern: pink, aqua, melon, and sunshine yellow indicate that this is a child's print. Fall 1948.

The story of Jack and Jill is depicted in this child's print. Pale aqua. Available, not shown, in pale baby pink, pale mint green, pale yellow, and very light dawn gray. Spring 1949.

Children at play, box layout with brushstroke stripes, in pastel pinks, blues, and beige. Spring 1949.

Children's stories including Little Red Hen, Puss 'n' Boots, and Jack & Jill. Cotton chintz. Spring 1949.

Tiny nautical motifs with stars and stripes. Spring 1941.

NOVELTY: NAUTICAL/PATRIOTIC

New Low Price on a Winner!
$1.98
Value $2.98

THE FAMOUS CALIFORNIA
Matletex
REG. U. S. PAT. OFF.

4 STAR FEATURE

Play Dress with Panties Attached

Sears 4-Star Feature Because:
★ Famous proven-success fashion . . a favorite on the playgrounds of the nation.
★ Exclusive with Sears! No other mail-order house sells it or can sell it.
★ Fits beautifully because the Lastex-shirred Matletex adjusts to your figure-size.
★ Perfect all-in-one play dress; complete in itself; eliminates underclothes!

Whirl-skirt play dress with bodice and

Junior Jury **Playmates**

Colors gay as sunshine . . .

Two to Team-up!
69¢ $1.00
Shirt   Overall

3-Pc. Sailor Su
$1.98 Set
Choice of 2 Fabrics

Ⓐ Classic Shirt, Convertible   Ⓑ Shipshape In-or-o

Above: From *Sears Catalog*, Spring and Summer 1941, Philadelphia, Edition 182, ©

Left: Nautical theme with sailboats, anchors, and wheels. The stars lend a patriotic feel to the design. Spring 1941.

Right: Large monotone print of navy and airforce planes, navy blue. Not shown: flag red, and cadet blue. Cotton chintz. Spring 1942.

One of many nautical designs popular during this period, this print features sailors and tropical islands in a clearly military motif. White on navy. Spring 1941.

Nautical flags and wheels in red, white and blue. Spring 1941.

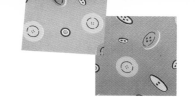

Right: Scattered tossed buttons on horizon blue. Also in pink, aqua, yellow, and gray. Fall 1948.

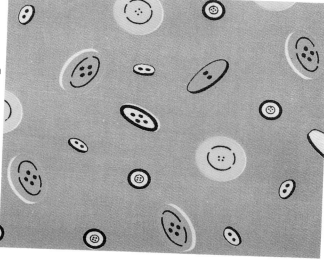

Novelty: Whimsical

Floating cameos in a blue background. Also shown: pale pink and desert sand. Softer shades of pastel were the new colors at decade's end. The trend continued into the early half of the 1950s. Spring 1949.

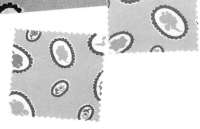

Above: An assortment of keys tossed on a blue field. Not shown: pink, aqua, sunshine yellow, and French gray. Spring 1949.

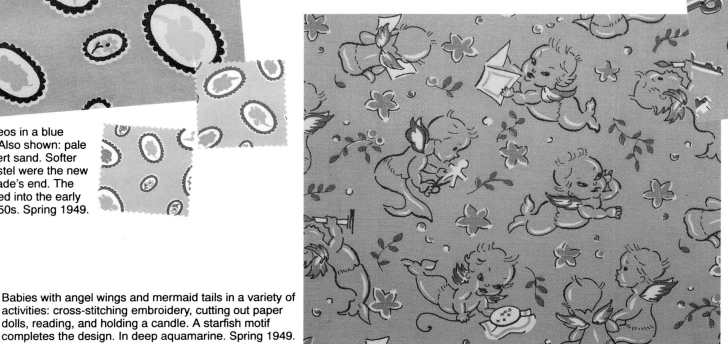

Babies with angel wings and mermaid tails in a variety of activities: cross-stitching embroidery, cutting out paper dolls, reading, and holding a candle. A starfish motif completes the design. In deep aquamarine. Spring 1949.

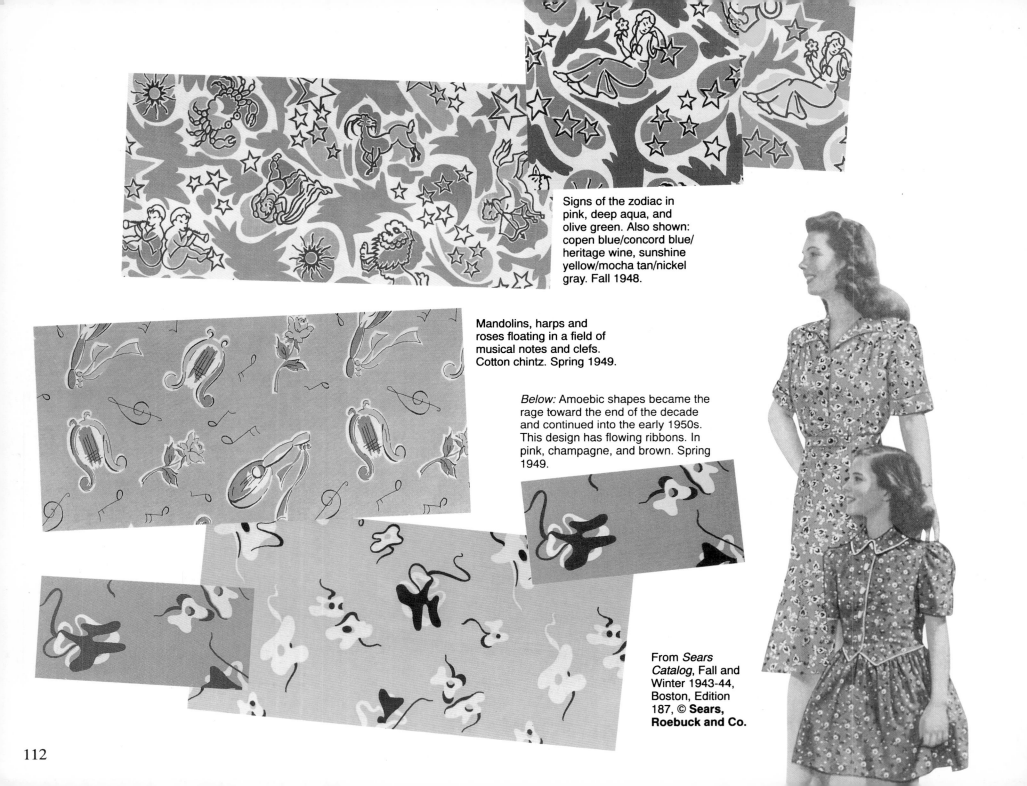

Signs of the zodiac in pink, deep aqua, and olive green. Also shown: copen blue/concord blue/ heritage wine, sunshine yellow/mocha tan/nickel gray. Fall 1948.

Mandolins, harps and roses floating in a field of musical notes and clefs. Cotton chintz. Spring 1949.

Below: Amoebic shapes became the rage toward the end of the decade and continued into the early 1950s. This design has flowing ribbons. In pink, champagne, and brown. Spring 1949.

From *Sears Catalog*, Fall and Winter 1943-44, Boston, Edition 187, © **Sears, Roebuck and Co.**

112